All Wrappe In Paracoru

Knife and Tool Wraps, Survival Bracelets, And More Projects With Parachute Cord

Nicholas Tomihama

All Wrapped Up in Paracord

Levi Dream

Copyright © 2013 Nicholas Tomihama

www.backyardbowyer.com

Printed in the United States of America

First Printing in 2013

ISBN : 978-1483969169

For Angela, Levi, and Noah

David was greatly distressed because the men were talking of stoning him; each one was bitter in spirit because of his sons and daughters.

But David found strength in the Lord his God.

- 1 Samuel 30 : 6

About the Author

Nicholas Tomihama is the author of *Adventures in Paracord* as well as several books on archery including *The Backyard Bowyer* and *Take-Down Archery*. He is an avid archer and bowyer who enjoys spending time outdoors with his family.

With his books and over 200 instructional videos Youtube channel (http://www.youtube.com/BackyardBowyer), he has spread his love of archery and making things. Nick is the originator of the tapered PVC pipe bow.

Nick grew up with Paracord and is no stranger to it. As an amateur knifemaker and collector of Japanese swords, he has always been fascinated by cord wrapping and

He lives with his wife and children in Honolulu, Hawaii on the island of Oahu.

Acknowledgements

First and foremost, I would like to thank you the reader for your time and support. Without you, all this would be for naught. Plus it would be like talking to myself in a very complicated, picture-intensive way. That would be pretty weird.

Thanks to all of my friends and supporters who have given me feedback in all forms. The praise has inspired me, the criticism has grounded me. In the end, this book would not have been possible without your help.

I want to thank my wife and two young sons, my guiding light and often the driving force behind many sleepless nights (working of course). Without you, I would have no reason to work hard and get anything done.

To my family, who have always been supportive of me and my dreams. Especially when they aren't exactly sure what it is I'm doing. If it makes you guys feel any better, I'm not exactly sure what it is I'm doing either.

God. When I have lost hope and allowed myself to wander, your guidance (sometimes not very pleasant guidance) has brought be back. Thank you for all the blessings in my life. Even the less than friendly ones.

Table of Contents

Chapter One
Getting Started

Welcome to <u>All Wrapped Up In Paracord</u>! In this chapter we'll go over some basic tools and materials needed to get started working with Paracord.

The first section is all about what Paracord is. We'll go over what different ratings and numbers mean and how they compare to each other. This section also explains the parts that make up Paracord as well as how to identify different grades and types of cord.

In the next section, we'll look at some basic tools and materials and how they are used in working with Paracord. Even complex projects can be done with only a few tools.

Alright, let's get started!

Getting Started
What is Paracord?

Paracord or parachute cord was originally developed for use in parachutes by the US military in WWII. The tough nylon rope was meant to replace silk, an expensive and scarce natural fiber. Once on the ground, so to speak, soldiers found nearly unlimited uses for the rot and water-resistant rope.

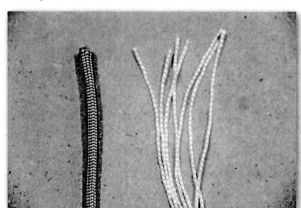

Paracord is a kernmantle rope. It is composed of a woven shell with a fiber core. The shell protects the inner strands from abrasion.

Since then, it has exploded in popularity among all branches of the military in the US and abroad as well as among civilians for a range of applications.

Paracord is a kernmantle rope, meaning it is composed of an inner core of threads or fibers that are encased in a woven shell. The core provides a great deal of the rope's tensile strength and can vary among types of cord. Because of its popularity, there are many different types of paracord available commercially.

There is paracord manufactured to government specifications, known as Mil-Spec (or MIL-C-5040) paracord. There are also civilian variants that are made to be similar to Mil-Spec but are different and have very different properties.

When I was first exposed to paracord it was Mil-Spec Type III in olive drab. This was true military surplus stuff, used by my father all his life. By the time I really got interested with paracord in college it was already difficult to find Mil-Spec cord. What I came across was a mix of Mil-Spec Type II and Type III, civilian Paraline, 450, and 550 cord. These are the main types of cord that usually fall into the category of paracord.

These all share a similar mantle or

This is the first paracord bracelet I built, back in college. It's made of Mil-Spec III with a backpack buckle.

shell, though the type of weave and diameter may vary. For the most part, this shell has a tensile strength of around 200 pounds. Mil-Spec Type II and 450 cord are similar in that their cores when combined with the shell have a tensile strength of around 450 pounds, hence 450 cord. Mil-Spec Type III and 550 cord are both in the 550 pound range for tensile strength. Paraline, while called 650 cord, only has a tensile strength

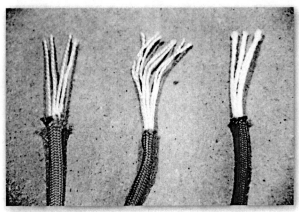

From left to right: 450, 550, and 650 cord.

of around 350 or less and can vary quite a bit.

When wrapping or making knots with paracord, the first thing to note is that for all intents and purposes, all of the basic types from 450 to 650 use the same shell. If you gut or take the core out of the paracord, it really doesn't matter what you start with. If you have a certain purpose in mind or want to use full cord, the different types have different characteristics.

450 cord is a more deflated cord and lays flatter than the others. This cord usually contains 4 tightly twisted strands of nylon in the core. It is great for low profile wraps where some body is required. It can be tricky to find, so one way to get the same look as 450 cord is to remove a little less than half of the internal strands of 550 cord.

550 cord is a good all-around cord for tying and wrapping. This cord has 7 tightly twisted internal nylon strands, though some commercial variants can have as few as 5. It is the best choice for items that will be used as the cord is very useful both as a whole and in parts. It's very strong, though commercial versions can vary quite a bit in actual tensile strength and uniformity.

Mil-Spec 550 is tough and suitable for use in situations where life or safety are at stake. Its 7 finely twisted 3-ply internal strands also have myriad uses on their own and can be used for lashing and tying by themselves. True Mil-Spec cord should have a tracer yarn that is a different color than the rest for identification purposes.

650 cord is a fuller cord with a softer feel. It is great for jewelry and crafts as the fuller body makes it more uniform in diameter and easier to work with. The

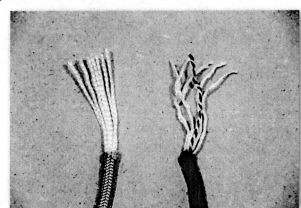

550 cord on the left, true Mil-Spec Type III with tracer yarn on the right.

fullness of it comes from the core which can range from 4 loosely twisted yarns to a loose fiber fill. Some of the downsides of 650 cord is that it can stretch much more than 550 cord and can deform when wet. It's not the best cord for practical applications.

There are also two other types of cord, type I and IV. Type I cord is a very thin cord with around 100 pounds of tensile strength. It makes a good cord for finer wraps and ties while retaining the look of paracord. Type IV is a very large cord and is often known as 750 cord, which is its tensile strength. It is a very strong cord and is great for wrapping larger items.

Getting Started
Tools and Supplies

Working with paracord can be a fun and rewarding hobby. In this book we'll be doing projects that can be worked on virtually anywhere and require only a few tools.

When I started working with paracord, all I really had was a knife, ruler, and lighter. Today my kit consists of a pair of scissors, knife, lighter, tape measure, lacing needle, superglue, and a few different colors of paracord. Here are few things that will help you when working with paracord.

Paracord
The first thing you'll need is some cord to work with. Paracord can be found at many sporting good, outdoor, hardware, and military surplus stores.

It can also be found online from various retailers, wholesalers, and on auction sites.

Keep in mind that some commercial Paracord is made of non-nylon fibers.

Cutting Tool
I like to have both a fine cutting tool like a razorblade or very sharp knife and a rough cutting tool like a pair of scissors.

The fine blade will be used for trimming ends flush and for precision cutting. The scissors are manly for cutting sections of cord to length.

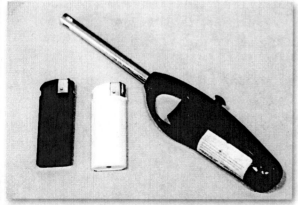

Lighter
A lighter or micro/pencil torch is invaluable for melting and singeing the ends of cord to prevent fraying.

The high heat of a micro torch is great for simply singeing the ends of cords as well as melting cord to fuse the ends. A lighter will only melt cord.

A hot-knife or metal-tipped craft/wood burner can also singe cord.

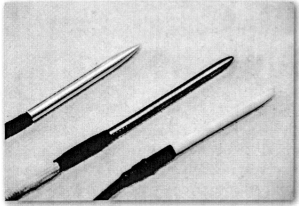

Lacing Needle

This tool, which can be considered and used like a fid and marlinspike, makes working with paracord much easier. It can be used to thread paracord into knots or under wraps, break and pry open knots, and to tighten up and finish knots or wraps.

We'll go over how to make a lacing needle in the next chapter.

Sealer

Sometimes a wrap or knot needs to be permanent. If that's the case, paracord can be soaked in some sort of sealer to harden it and make it permanent.

Liquid wood stabilizer is my favorite for larger wraps. CA glue, also known as super glue, is great for smaller applications such as sealing knots or as a no-heat way to keep ends from fraying.

Other Cord

While the main subject of this book is paracord, all the wraps and projects will work with any similar rope. Other synthetic kernmantle ropes like diamond braid nylon and polyester will look similar.

The wraps and knots in this book can also be done with natural ropes and cords as well.

Another tool that is useful to have is a measuring device. I like to have both a short ruler and a measuring tape in my kit as well as a yard or meter stick for my work space. This will be used for both measuring cord and for figuring out wrap lengths and for calculating cord amounts.

Keep a notebook or some way to record measurements on hand. The amount of cord needed for certain wraps and ties will change depending on the brand of cord, how tight you tie, and the way you prefer to finish projects. It's good to take information down as you work so you have good information to reference when planning future projects.

The measurements and cord lengths in this book should be used as a general guide. The best measurements will come from your own experiences and trials.

Chapter Two
Knots and Techniques

     This chapter contains a few useful knots and techniques that will be used repeatedly in this book. These basic knots, methods, and tools are some that I use most often and really can't live without. Once mastered, they will give you some options when tackling a new project and allow for clean, professional results.

     Below are a couple terms that will pop up repeatedly in this chapter and the rest of the book. For a full list of terms, you can check out the glossary on page 143.

     <u>Working Part / End</u> - The part of the cord that is involved in tying and wrapping.

     <u>Standing Part / End</u> - The part of the cord that is not used in wrapping or tying and is usually unfinished.

| Knots | 12 | Techniques | 27 |

Knots and Techniques
Knots

In this section we will cover four basic knots, each of them suited for a different purpose.

The overhand and lanyard knots are both great stopper knots for bracelets and lanyards. They can also be used on smaller wraps and are a great way to finish loose ends.

The Turk's head knot is a very versatile knot. It can be used as a large stopper knot, a decorative topper, a start and finish to wraps, and even a wrap in its own right.

As a way to shorten long dangling cord ends while wrapping or tying, the chain sinnet can't be beat. It is also the basis for a family of survival bracelets.

Knots

Overhand

One of the most basic of knots is the overhand knot, also known as a thumb knot. The difference in name comes from the way it is tied, whether over the hand or with the thumb. It is a very old knot and the basis for many others.

While simple, it is very effective in tying up loose ends because the knot jams or locks very badly. Combined with melting the ends, the overhand is simple and very hard to take apart.

This knot can be used as a stopper, a toggle for the end of a bracelet or lanyard, or even as a separator between different knots or wraps.

Start with your cord. The working end is on the top. This can be done with one strand or many.

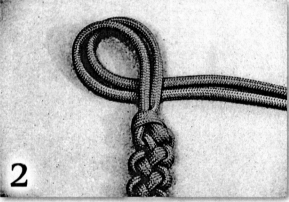

Take all strands and create a loop by bringing the working end under the main cord.

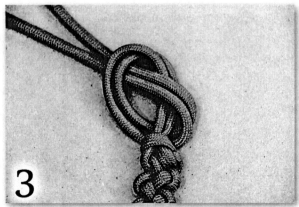

Either reach in and pull the working end over the main cord and through the loop (overhand) or push the working end over the main cord and through the loop (thumb).

Adjust the knot by pulling the working and standing ends until the knot is in the proper place. Then pull both very tight, jamming the cord and finishing the knot.

Knots

Lanyard

Also known as a diamond knot, the lanyard knot has a very neat and finished appearance that makes it perfect as an end toggle or a knot to separate a series of knots or wraps. While a little more complicated than the overhand, it is symmetrical and ends up being fuller.

It can be a little difficult to get at first, but once understood it is very simple. It is one of my favorite knots and my go-to knot for finishing up lanyards, bracelets, and for putting anywhere I need an attractive stopper knot.

To help you get this knot, we'll tie it in both double and single colors.

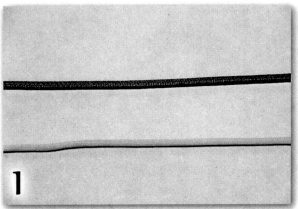

Start with your two color cords side by side with the working ends on the right. We will call the black cord A and the white cord B.

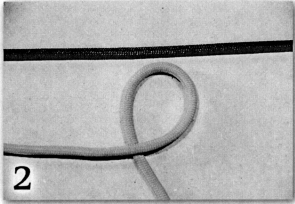

Bring the end of B under itself to form a loop.

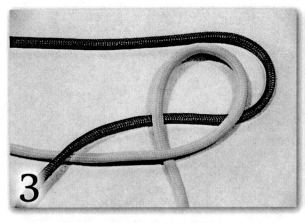

Pass A underneath but not through the loop and then over the starting end of B.

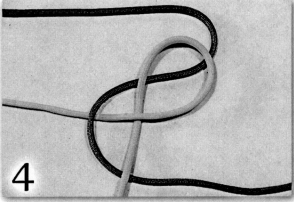

Pass A underneath the end of B.

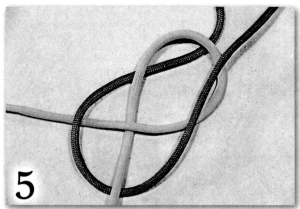

Bring the end of A over the looped formed by B.

Pass the end of A under itself and over the loop made by B. The two cords should now looks like two loops that are woven together.

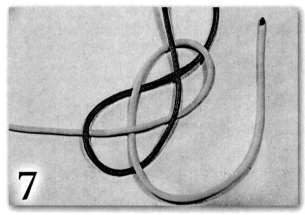

Bring the end of B around the main body of the knot.

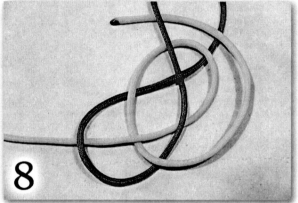

Pass the end of B over the starting side of A and under the working end of A.

Reach into the center diamond-shaped hole of the knot and pull the end of B through.

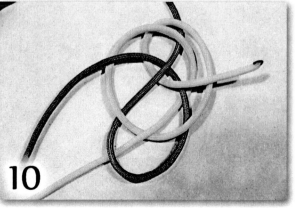

Take the end of A and bring it around the main body of the knot.

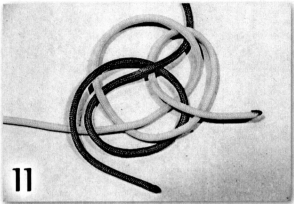

The end of A should go over the start of B.

Reach into the center of the knot and pull the end of A through.

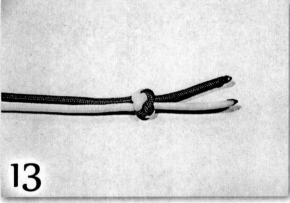

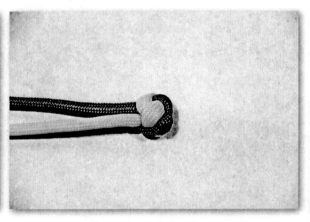

Pull both ends and work out the slack until a tight knot forms. It helps to work on both cords equally so that the knot is well formed, otherwise the knot may look wrong.

Here's the finished knots with the working ends trimmed and melted.

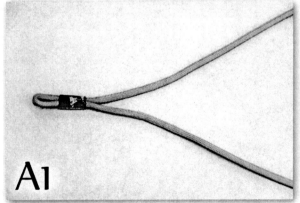

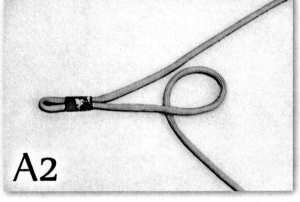

The lanyard knot is great as a stopper for loops. Start by tying or taping the cord just below where the loop ends. We will call the top cord A and the bottom cord B.

Bring the end of B under itself to form a loop.

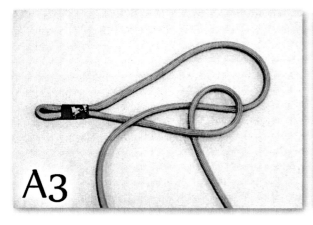

Pass A underneath but not through the loop and then over the starting end of B.

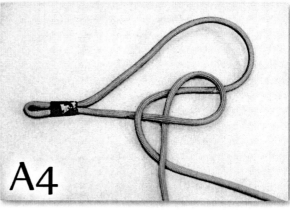

Pass A underneath the end of B.

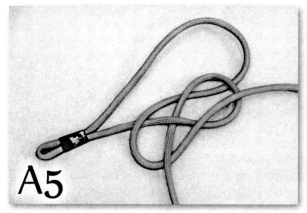

Bring the end of A over the looped formed by B.

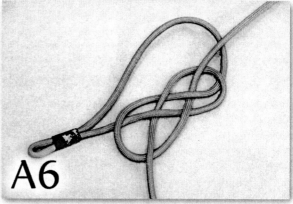

Pass the end of A under itself and over the loop made by B. The two cords should now looks like two loops that are woven together.

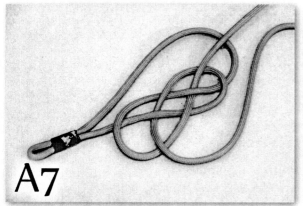

Bring the end of B around the main body of the knot.

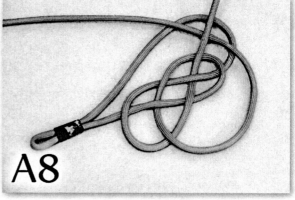

Pass the end of B over the starting side of A and under the working end of A.

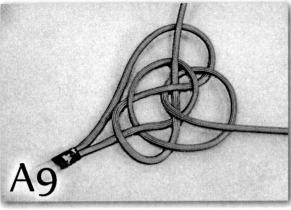

Reach into the center diamond-shaped hole of the knot and pull the end of B through.

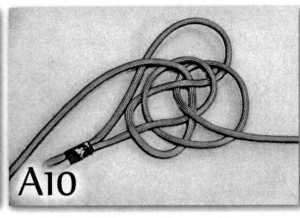

Take the end of A and bring it around the main body of the knot.

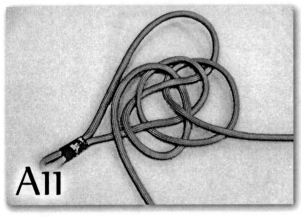

The end of A should go over the start of B.

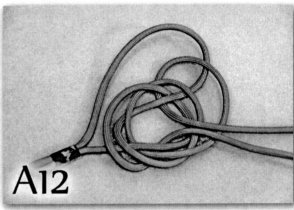

Reach into the center of the knot and pull the end of A through.

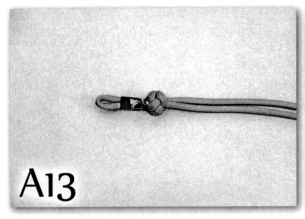

Pull both ends and work out the slack until a tight knot forms. It can take a bit of work to get the knot to form right at first.

Here's the finished knot with the tape on the loop removed.

Knots

Turk's Head

The Turk's head is a decorative knot that can have many uses. It's my favorite way to start and end wraps because of how clean and finished it looks. This is also a great knot for hiding parts of a wrap or another knot. It can also be placed in the middle of some wraps to add body or create a separate section like a handle or grip area.

It's also great on its own as a topper for walking sticks, knife handles, hammer heads, and anywhere else a decorative touch is welcome. The Turk's head can also be tied one after another to become a comfortable and attractive wrap in its own right.

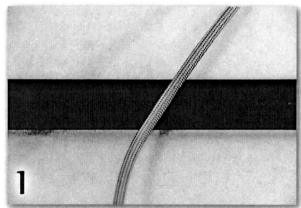

Start by placing your cord over the handle. The working end is to the right. I suggest using a longer cord to tie this knot as the excess can be pulled through and saved later.

Bring the working end around the back of the handle and then cross it over itself.

After crossing over the front, pass the working end over the back of the handle again.

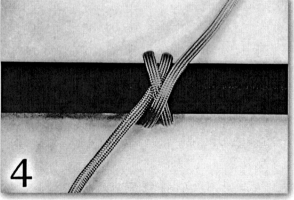

Bring the working end up between the standing end and the first loop, then cross over the first loop.

Pass the working end under the standing end. It should look like this with the working end pointing up and the standing end pointing down.

Flip the handle over. The working end should now be pointing down and the standing end should be pointing up.

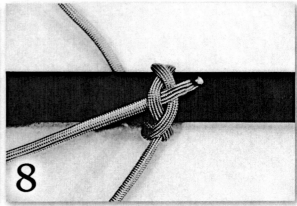

Take the left loop and pull it over the right loop. Be sure to only overlap them slightly and do not completely pull the left loop over the right.

Push the working end under the bottom loop.

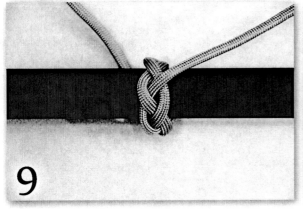

Pull the working end all the way through. You can start to see the weaving pattern at this point.

Push the working end under the top portion of the right loop. You are basically going under the same loop in step 8, just after the overlap.

11

Pull the working end all the way through,

12

Give the handle about a 1/4 turn. At this point, if the handle is larger and needs more body, repeat steps 6-11 to add another set of woven loops.

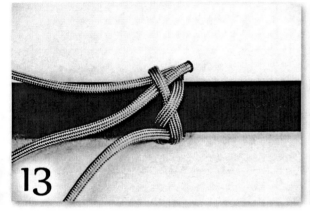

13

To finish up the first layer of the knot, start by pushing the working end under the same loop the standing end is under.

14

Pull the working end through to finish up the first pass. The knot can be tightened at this point or bulked up by making multiple passes.

15

Start the second pass by following the first loop and pushing the working end under the same loop. You want to basically lay the new cord next to the cord from the first pass.

16

Pull the cord through. You can see that now there are two cords going under the same loop.

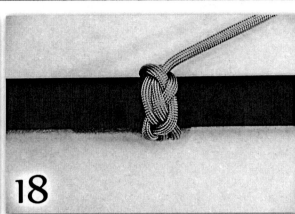

Follow the cord from the first pass and push the working end under the same loop. Keep in mind that the new cord stays on the same side.

Pull the cord through. You can see it lays down to the right of the original pass. Keep the new cord on the right side as you go to keep the knot uniform

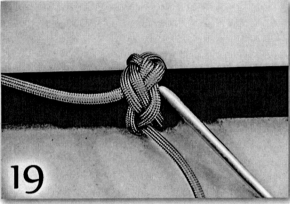

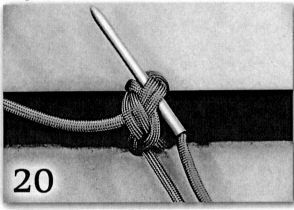

Continue following the cord from the first pass. Once the loops end up doubled, I like using a lacing needle to speed things up. You could also work some slack into the knot..

Push the needle under the two loops. A blunt needle works best for this type of work.

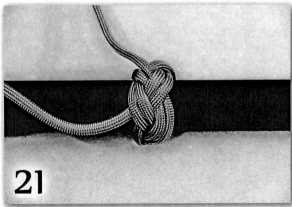

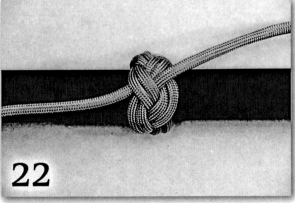

Pull the working end all the way through and continue following the original pass.

Push the working end under the starting loop once you've finished this pass. At this point you can either continue adding passes or finish the knot.

The easiest way to tighten up the knot is to start back at the beginning of the knot. Pull on the standing end until you have enough loose cord to work with.

Pull the slack under the loop and use the extra cord to tighten the cord down.

Continue tightening the knot, working on one section at a time until the whole knot is tightened.

Here's the knot tightened and finished. The standing end can go on to become the basis for a wrap or row of knots.

Here's the knot with both ends trimmed and melted. The melted ends were then pulled into the wrap while still hot, locking them in place. A drop of glue can also lock the knot.

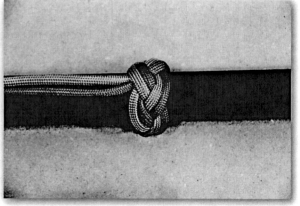

Here's the Turk's head done in one pass with two cords. This is a good way to start double cord wraps or doubled single cord wraps.

Knots

Chain Sinnet

The chain sinnet is a very interesting and useful knot. Also known by many names including monkey braid, chain stitch, crochet stitch, finger crochet, daisy chain, and others. It is a useful method for shortening a cord and can allow a length of rope to be stored without tangling. I use it to shorten the working ends of cord as I wrap.

It's best feature is that it can be completely unravelled easily. When the working end is pulled, the loops pull out of the previous loops and the whole thing comes apart cleanly. This makes it useful for keeping emergency cord handy.

I will admit I've spent hours tying and unravelling this knot. It's addictive.

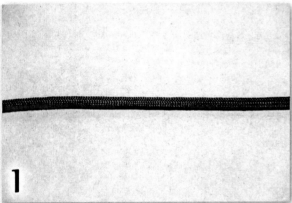

Start with a length of cord. The standing end is to the left and the working end is to the right.

Make a loop with the cord by passing the working end under the main cord. We are basically starting an overhand knot.

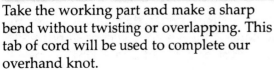

Take the working part and make a sharp bend without twisting or overlapping. This tab of cord will be used to complete our overhand knot.

Press or pull the tab of cord through the loop as if making an overhand knot.

Tighten the knot by pulling both the standing end and the tab. Because the knot is secured to the tab, pulling the working end through will cause the knot to undo itself.

Make a second tab with the working part.

Press or pull the tab through the loop made by the first tab.

Tighten the knot by pulling on the tab. Each future knot will be the same as this one we just finished.

Continue the chain by making another tab and passing it through the loop.

Pull the tab to tighten the knot.

Keep on creating knots until you reach the desired length of your chain. This knot can be modified to make bracelets like on page 114.

When tied loosely, the chain sinnet can be used to store short lengths of cord or prevent tangling.

The two pieces of paracord in the picture are the same length.

The chain sinnet makes the cord appear much shorter. This makes working with and storing longer lengths of cord.

The Turk's head knot makes for a very attractive start and finish for wraps.

A single Turk's head is great for keeping the wrap one thickness as it does not add much to the ends.

Two or more passes give the knot more body, making it perfect as a topper or for creating boundaries on a handle or bar.

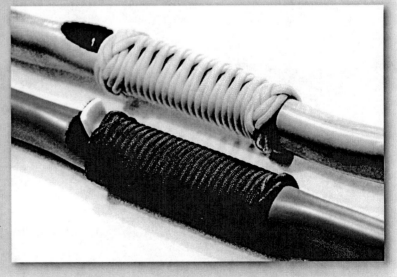

Knots and Techniques

Techniques

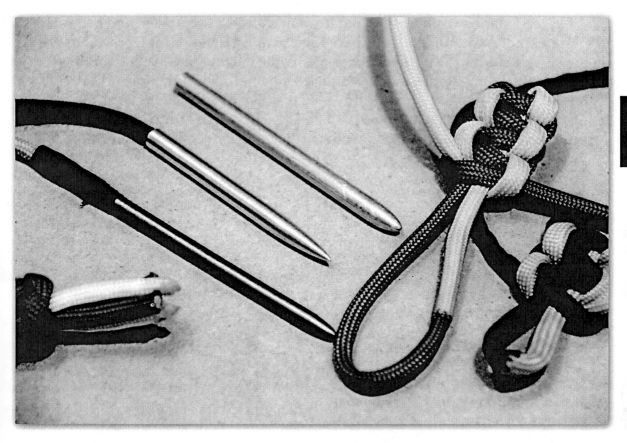

In this section we'll go over making a lacing needle or fid, sealing and fusing paracord with heat, and splicing multiple cords together.

In chapter one we talked about the lacing needle. This is a versatile and compact tool that works as a fid and marlinspike. It's great for wrapping and tying tight and consistently as well as removing even jammed knots with ease.

Being made of nylon, Paracord melts into a hard plastic when heated to the right temperature. Singeing loose ends can keep them from unravelling and melted cord can act as a glue, fusing parts of a wrap together.

On wraps that make use of a single length of cord, splicing two or more colors together gives any project more contrast and variety.

Techniques

Making a Lacing Needle

When I started working with paracord in college, I used pliers and hemostats to tuck and pull cord through tight spaces and to finish up knots. It worked but there was still much to be desired. Years later while delving into leatherworking I discovered the lacing needle and haven't used a pair of pliers for paracord since.

A lacing needle has a hollow threaded end that holds onto the cord and a pointed end that works like the point of a needle. This tool can also be called a fid or paracord needle. It has a few uses including threading paracord, opening knots, and tightening knots. It can also be made with a solid rod and function like a marlinspike.

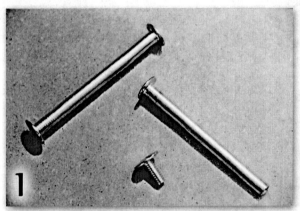

Most hardware stores carry 1/4" aluminum screw posts or binding posts. A good length for a lacing needle is 3-4 inches. Remove the threaded screw from the post.

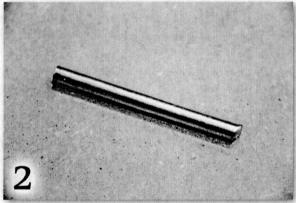

Cut the head off of the post. Because the aluminum is fairly soft, this can be done with most saws, tin snips, or bolt cutters.

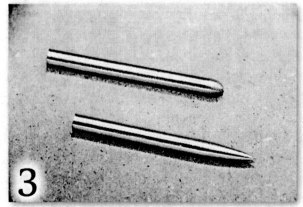

Grind the solid end to a point with a file, sandpaper, or grinder. A rounded point works well for most applications. A sharp point is great for taking jammed knots apart.

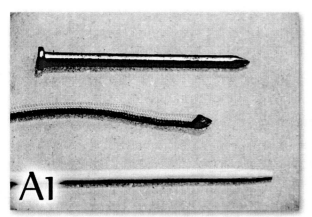

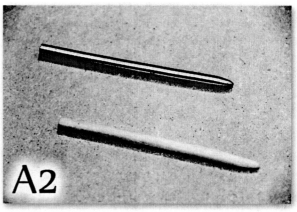

Another style of lacing needle can be made with a solid rod. A nail and bamboo skewer are pictured, but anything that is roughly the diameter of paracord will work.

Simply cut the needle to length and shape the tip.

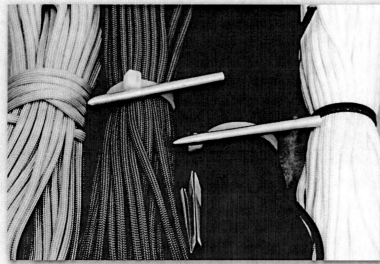

The blunt needle is a great all-around needle for general knot work. It's also great for nudging open tough knots without fraying the cord or scratching underneath.

Sharp needles are a must for taking apart jammed knots or working very tight knots. Keep in mind they have a tendency to mar surfaces.

A lacing needle is invaluable for working with Turk's head knots.

This single-pass knot was done without any extra tightening by using a lacing needle.

It's difficult to get the tight braided look that a balanced Turk's head knot has without a lacing needle or similar tool.

Techniques

Attaching Needle

A lacing needle that locks over the end of the cord works really well for tight spaces and general wrapping and knot work. The needle transitions smoothly to the cord, allowing very tight knots and wraps to be done without the cord getting stuck or pulled free from the needle.

A needle that does not lock can be used for looser knots and wraps. It's also for attaching cord to a needle that is fixed and cannot be attached in any other way.

We'll go over how to prep cord for attaching to a needle as well as some alternative attaching methods for improvised needles or marlinspikes.

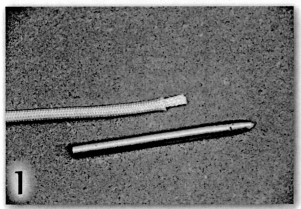

Start with the hollow-ended needle and the end of your paracord.

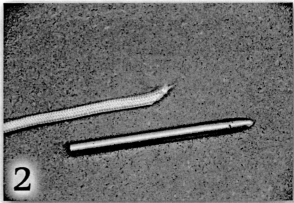

Cut the end of the cord at a 30 to 40 degree angle. This will give a nice taper that will allow the cord to fit into the needle.

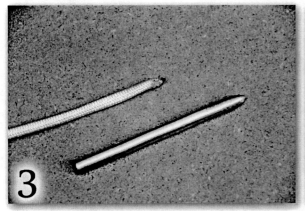

Burn the end of the cord so that it melts and forms a tapered blob. Make sure that the smallest end of the taper still fits into the end of the needle.

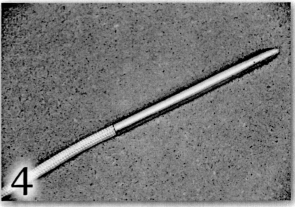

Once cool, twist the needle over the end of the paracord. The internal threads will cut into the plastic giving a firm grip.

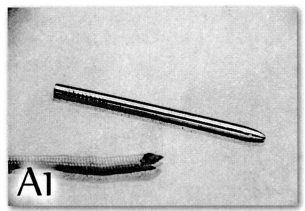

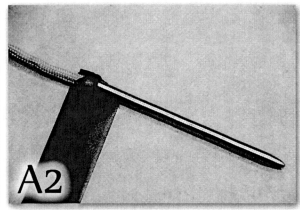

This method works well if the solid-ended needle you are using is the same diameter or larger than your paracord. Start by melting the end of the cord.

Line the cord up with the needle. A roughly 2 inch strip of tape will hold both together. Duct tape and electrical tape work well.

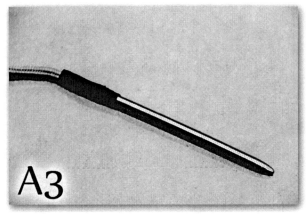

Wrap the tape tightly around the joint and the needle is ready for use.

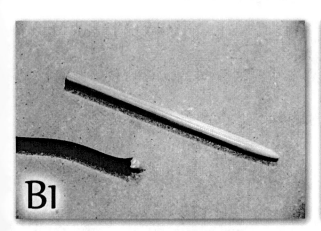

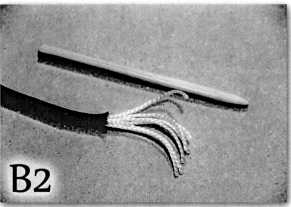

If your needle is smaller than your paracord, this method works well. Cut the end of the cord so that the shell has a nice clean edge.

Pull about an inch of the core out of the end. Do this lightly so that the shell will easily slide back in place.

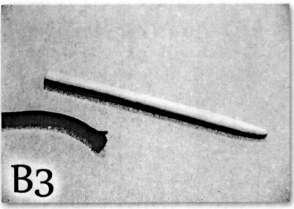

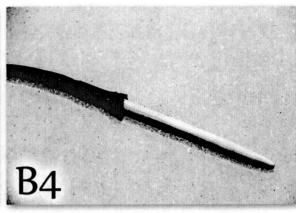

Cut the core and slide the shell back up so that there is a roughly one inch empty space in the end of the cord.

Slide the needle into the end of the cord until it pushes into the core.

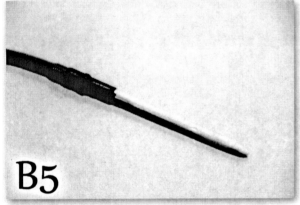

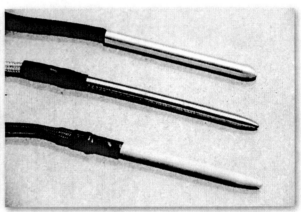

Wrap the end of the cord tightly with a little bit of tape. If your needle is metal, you can simply melt the shell onto the needle and then use heat to break it off later.

Here are the three styles of attachment. Of the three, the threaded needle is the best for working with knots like the Turk's head.

This watch band was done with two layers of cobra knots with gutted Paracord.

When working with knots that are very tight or packed closely together, a lacing needle or marlinspike is invaluable.

Techniques

Melting Ends

Paracord, because it is made of nylon, melts and fuses together like plastic when heated enough. This makes sealing the ends to prevent fraying, locking knots together, and fusing cord to surfaces fairly straightforward.

In section A we'll go over melting the ends of cord to keep the ends from fraying. This method can also be used to harden or reshape the end of a length of cord for threading into holes or as a short improvised lacing needle.

Section B is all about heating cord and fusing it into the cord around it. This method is great for finishing a variety of wraps and knots quickly and securely.

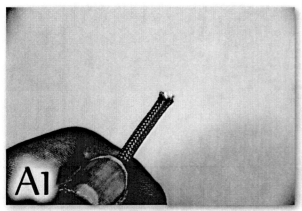

Cut the end of your cord so that there is a clean edge.

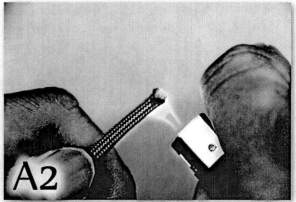

Heat the end with a lighter. The nylon will start to melt into a blob of plastic.

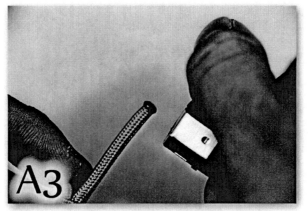

Take the heat away and a small bead will form on the end. The high-heat of a micro or pencil torch will sear the end and produce less of a bead.

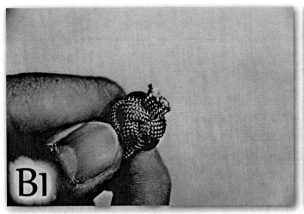

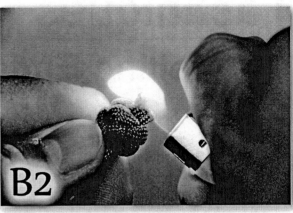

To finish the end of a knot, start by trimming the ends with a sharp knife. This should be roughly 1/8 to 1/4 of an inch.

Heat the end of the cord until it melts. Make sure to keep the flame from touching the knot or surrounding cord.

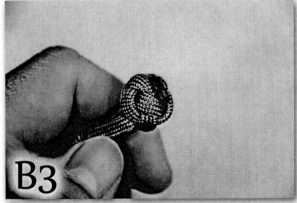

If you want to flatten the burned end or blend it into the rest of the cord, use the back or flat of a cold knife. A finger can also be used, but be careful and let the cord cool down just enough to prevent burns. An ice cube can also be used to quickly cool molten cord.

While not the prettiest way to finish a bracelet, melting and fusing the loose ends is a very sturdy method.

While it holds well, it can still be worked apart fairly easily if the bracelet needs to be unraveled.

Techniques

Two Cord Splice

Many wraps can be made more visually striking with two colors of Paracord. On single cord wraps and some double cord wraps, using two separate cords is an option. For some wraps and especially for bracelets and straps, the simplest way to get two colors is to splice two cords together.

While this splice is not very strong on its own, it is a very clean method of splicing cords together. With a little practice, multi-colored wraps can be achieved by splicing multiple cord colors or alternating colors together.

Treat a spliced cord as separate cords rather than a single cord strength-wise.

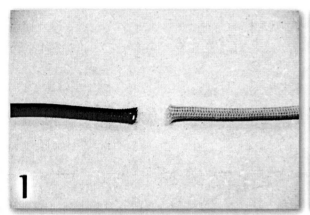

Cut the ends of the cords that will be spliced together. The cord on the left will be pushed into the cord on the right.

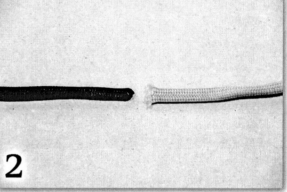

Melt the end of the cord on the left. Pull out and cut about an inch to two inches of core from the cord on the right. Pull the shell over so that the end of the cord is empty.

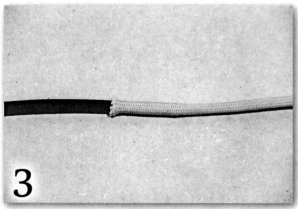

Push the melted cord into the empty cord. Make sure the inner cord goes all the way to the core strands of the other cord. If the cords are gutted this isn't important.

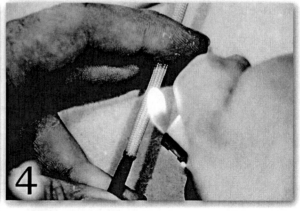

Gently heat the outer cord so that the cords fuse but not so much that they melt.

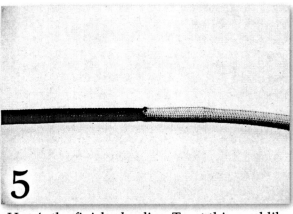

5

Here's the finished splice. Treat this cord like a single cord when using wraps, but keep in mind that the splice itself cannot bear any weight.

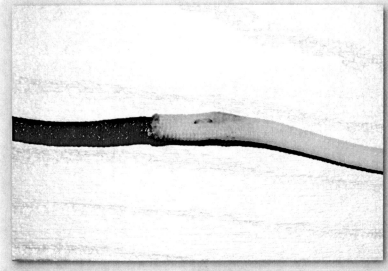

One way to increase the strength of a splice is to stitch the splice with a heavy-weight thread.

The inner nylon strands of 550 cord is perfect for this.

The only way to make a stronger splice is to slide two shells over one set of cords and have them meet at the middle.

When working with spliced cord, keep in mind where the splice is.

The cobra knot on the right will have a splice showing when the knot is finished.

The cobra knot on the left will have the splice hidden once the wrap is continued and completed.

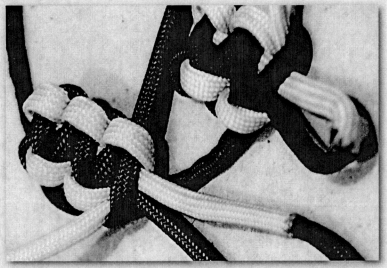

Chapter Three
Wraps

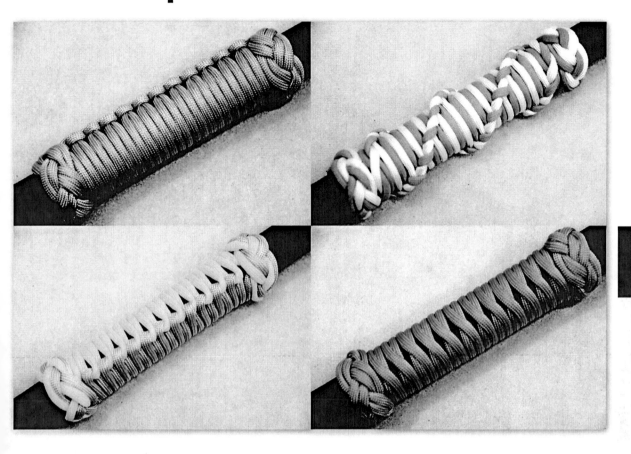

In this chapter we will be working on eight different wraps. They range from multi-use to specialized. The first section of this chapter is all about basic techniques for starting and finishing wraps.

The next two sections show how to perform different wraps and are grouped by the number of cords involved in the wrap. Single cord wraps only make use of a single working cord. Double cord wraps can either use a single cord with two working ends or two separate cords.

The wraps are also broken up into two categories. No knot wraps are not as secure, making them great for removable wraps. Knot based wraps are more secure and usually offer a more aggressive grip.

Wraps

Starting and Finishing

The key to durable and secure wraps is mastering starting and finishing. Without a strong and durable anchor, even the best wraps will easily come undone.

Mastering these techniques will allow you to adapt wraps to fit certain projects and circumstances. The styles of starting and finishing in this chapter will range from quick and easily removed to more elaborate and nearly permanent.

Starting and Finishing
Pull Through

The pull through method, also known as whipping, is a very simple way to start and finish a single cord wrap all in one. It makes use of a loop formed by the cord itself running under the whole wrap to secure both ends.

While it is mainly for applying basic wraps quickly, it can be used with other wrap styles. Keep in mind that with this wrap there will be a raised ridge where the equivalent of two cords will run under the handle.

When using this method for wraps that have openings or ridges, try to place the interior cords away from them as they will show through or make ridges uneven.

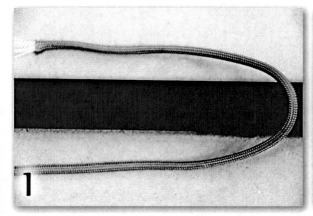

Start by making a U-shape with your cord. The standing end it at the top and the working end is at the bottom.

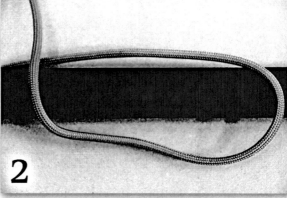

Bring the working end over the standing end where the wrap starts, forming a loop. The loop should be about an inch longer than the area to be wrapped.

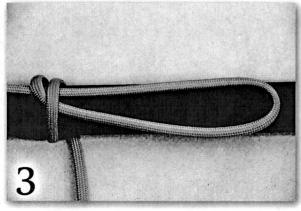

Bring the working end around the back of the handle and over itself and the rest of the loop.

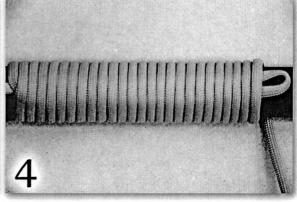

Pull the end tight and then continue wrapping until you reach the end of the handle.

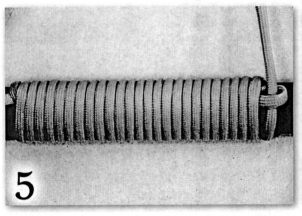

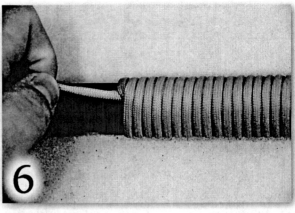

Pass the working end through the end of the loop.

Grip the standing end and pull it so that the loop is pulled part-way through. Don't pull it all the way or the wrap will unravel.

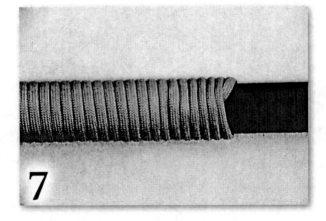

Once the end is pulled under, trim all the loose ends.

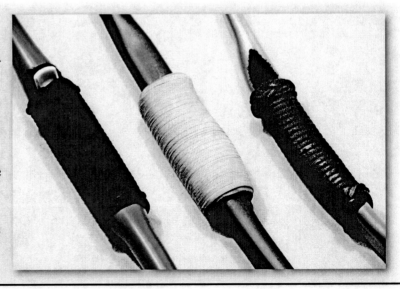

These three bow handles sport the basic wrap.

The two outer handles are started and finished with Turk's head knots.

The one on the left uses a single pass knot while the one on the right has two passes.

The center wrap uses the pull through method.

Starting and Finishing

Wrap Over

This method is great for starting single cord wraps as-is, or can be doubled to work with double-cord wraps. If used for two cord wraps, a two tone look can be achieved without using cord splices.

The method shown below uses a small length of cord under the wrap, though this can be extended for a more consistent handle feel. Like the other methods that hide portions of cord under the wrap, there will be a noticeable ridge.

One way to counter the ridge is to remove the core from the portion of cord that will be hidden under the wrap.

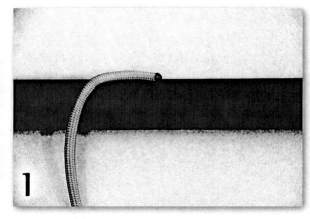

Start with the standing end placed next to the handle. It should be two or three inches long as it will hold the wrap together.

Bring the working end around the back of the handle and over the standing end.

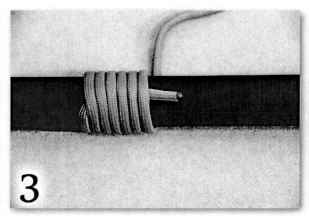

Tightly wrap over the standing end, locking it in place. Before it is completely covered, pull it tight to take any slack out of the top.

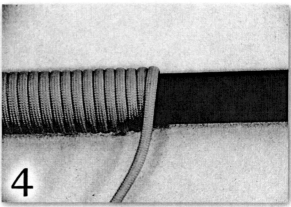

Once the standing end is covered by cord, the wrap can be finished with any other method.

Starting and Finishing

Loop

Like the name suggests, the loop method uses a separate loop of cord to pull the cord under itself. It's a great finishing method for both single and double cord wraps and can be made very secure.

This is my go to method for finishing permanent bracelets or wraps that will not be removed. For the best results, the loop cord and main cord should be of a similar diameter and should be equal as far as interior strands goes.

One way to make a very secure and clean finish without a ridge is to remove the interior of the loose end of the cord that will end up under the wrap.

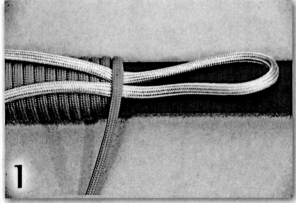

Start finishing the wrap once you're an inch or two away from the end. Take a secondary length of paracord about a foot long and lay it down over the wrap.

Wrap over the loop as if it wasn't there. If your wrap has an open area like the crossed back wrap, make sure the loop is in a covered area.

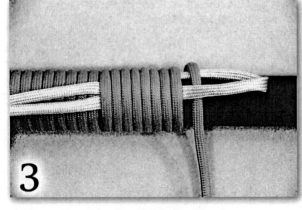

Once you've finished your wrap, pass the working end through the loop.

Pull on the loop and work it under the wrap.

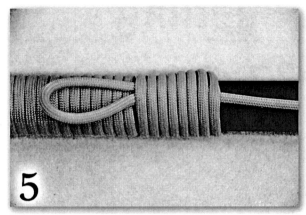

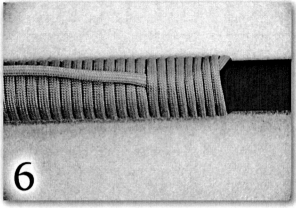

Pull on the loop until there is enough working end to get a good grip on. Pull it all the way through.

Go back and work out all of the slack from your wrap and pull the working end to tighten.

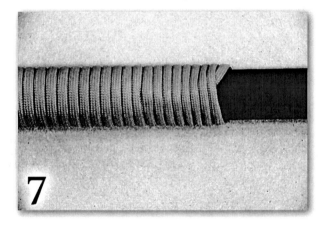

Once the wrap is secure, trim and hide the working end under the wraps.

These clubs have wrist loops to help give a better grip and to keep them attached to a wrist if they ever slip.

There are many ways to add loops under a wrap.

The loops can be an extension of the wrap like the looped method.

Another way is to wrap over the loose ends of the loops to secure them.

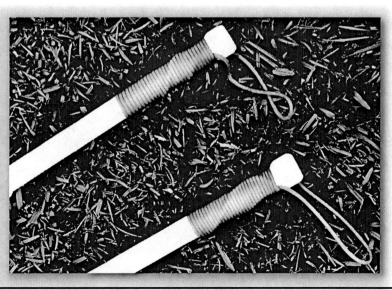

Starting and Finishing

Reverse Wrap

I like to call this method the reverse wrap. Not to be confused with the rope builder's term for making counter-twist rope, this wrap was inspired by a bowstring technique called backserving. It is used to cleanly and securely finish the ends of cord used to pad high-friction areas of a bowstring.

This method is great for finishing up any basic wrap, though it is nearly impossible to use this on other wrap styles. Due to the nature of the wrap, the end will end up looking like a basic wrap. This can be a nice effect, especially on wraps that alternate from one wrap style to another.

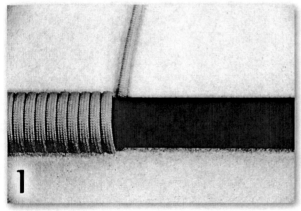

Start about an inch or two away from the end of the wrap.

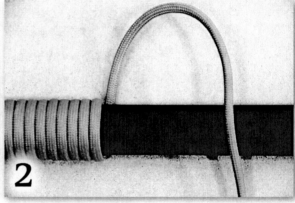

Bring the working end over the handle to form a fairly large loop.

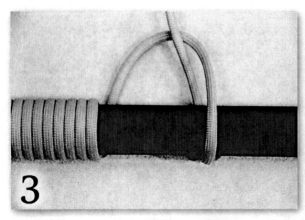

Take the working end and loop it around the handle and under the loop.

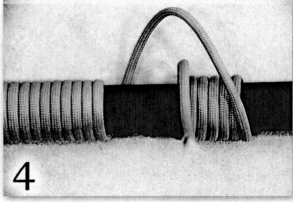

Start wrapping in reverse until there is about an inch or two of cord wrapped under the loop.

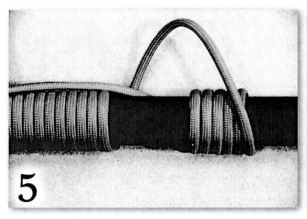

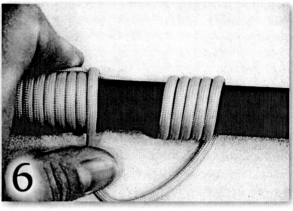

Take the working end and lay it alongside the main wrap, under the loop.

Use the loop to start wrapping. The reverse wrap you did will transfer over to the main wrap, covering the working end.

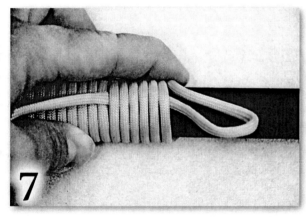

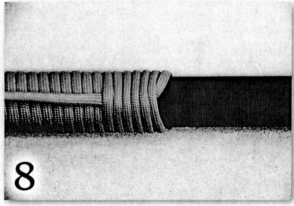

Once the loops are transferred over, make sure to tighten everything and work out any slack in the wrap.

Pull the working end to remove the slack and tighten the wrap.

Trim the working end to finish the wrap.

Starting and Finishing

Over Needle

This method of finishing wraps is really useful for getting a nice clean finish without re-wrapping or using loops. While it works best with single cord wraps, this method also works for double cord wraps if two needles are used instead of just one.

If there is no lacing needle available, a pencil or finger can be used to created space underneath the wrap. When the object is removed, the loose end of the cord can be pulled through and the wrap then tightened.

Once the cord has been pulled under the main wrap, the needle can then be used to assist in tightening the wrap. This is one of the more secure methods.

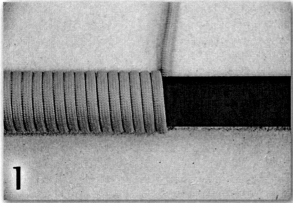

Start about an inch or two away from the end of the wrap.

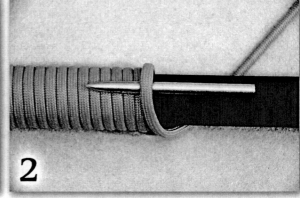

Place a lacing needle on the handle and begin wrapping over it. A pencil or other object can be used instead.

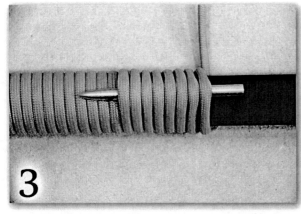

Wrap over the needle. If using a pencil or similar spacer, keep the wraps fairly loose.

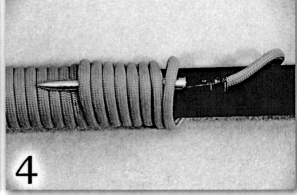

Once the wrap is finished, tape the working end to the end of the needle.

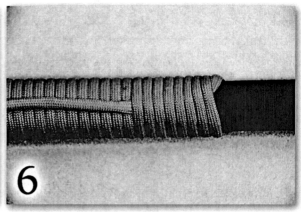

Pull the needle through and the working end along with it. If using a pencil or other spacer, pull the pencil out and pass the working end under the loops.

Work the slack out of the loops and pull the working end tight.

Trim the working end to finish the wrap.

This method can also be used to finish the ends of knotted wraps like the cobra knot.

Simply tie over the needle and then pull the working end through and work the slack out of the knots.

This results in a much cleaner finish than simply melting the ends.

Starting and Finishing

Knot and Melt

The simplest way to finish a knot-based wrap is to simply trim the loose ends and melt them into the wrap like the instructions below. This works because each knot in a knotted wrap is held in place by itself or another cord and the melted Paracord fuses, locking the end of the cord in place.

If a wrap has no knots, a simple one or a transition to a knot-based wrap can be used to lock the wrap enough to melt the cord in place. This method works equally well for single and double cords but may require two knots when being used for double cords.

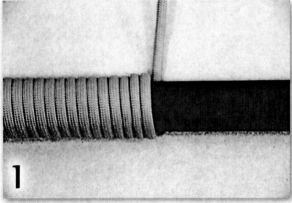

Finish wrapping and make sure everything is tight.

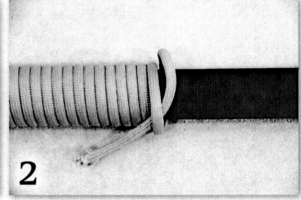

Take the working end and pass it under the last loop.

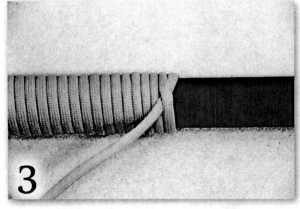

Pull the working end tight to lock the cord in place and secure the wrap.

Cut the end, leaving about 1/4 inch or cord. Melt the end and press it into the wrap to finish the knot.

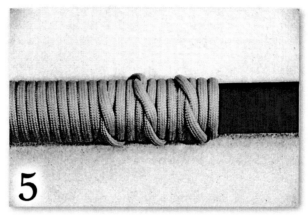

Another way to finish a non-knotted wrap is to transition to a knot-based wrap and melt the ends of the knot.

This bow handle was finished by melting the ends of the cord into the Turk's head knots at the ends.

While not as clean in appearance as ends that are glued and hidden, this method of finishing is very secure.

Handle wraps that get wet or are immersed in water stay together better when the ends are melted.

This is the tang end of a sword that was broken. A simple crossed back wrap over the tang of the blade turned this into one of the most useful machetes I've used in a while.

Sometimes even a simple Paracord wrap can turn broken knives or blades into useable tools quickly and safely.

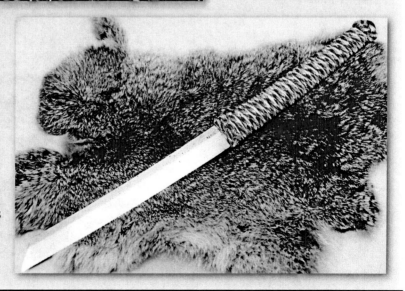

Starting and Finishing
Turk's Head

The Turk's head knot, which can be found on page 19, is a very versatile decorative knot. It creates an attractive weave and is perfect for starting and finishing wraps. Because it is a very secure knot, it can be used to start or finish any wrap style in double or single cord.

If a wrap needs separation or areas to add grip, the Turk's knot is a great option. Since the knot can be tied with only one working end, it can be tied multiple times within a wrap. Another option to add extra color is to tie separate Turk's head knots over starting and finishing ends or between section in a wrap.

Finish wrapping and make sure everything is tight.

Tie a Turk's head knot to finish the knot. A single pass will produce a fairly low-profile knot that rests close to the body of the wrap.

You could also add more passes for a little more body. A larger knot makes a great hand-stop for walking sticks and knives without a guard.

Starting and Finishing
Two End Start

Double cord knots can often be done with a single cord folded over. If a wrap is started in this way, there is no need for a separate knot or method to lock the cord onto the item to be wrapped. There are no loose ends on the starting end, making this very secure. This method is great for thinner wraps or wraps in places where a less secure staring method would unravel with use.

This simple method works best for double cord wraps. It can work on some double single cord wraps where the two wraps go in opposite directions. A good example of this can be found at the bottom of page 58.

Place the center of the cord under the handle.

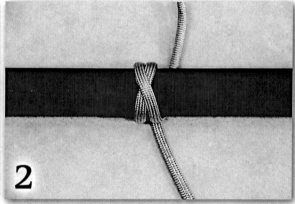

Start your wrap. The front of the wrap will look like this.

This wrap will have a single straight bar across the back at the start. From here continue wrapping until you reach the end.

Wraps
Single Cord

Single cord wraps make use of only one working end, making them great for open-ended wraps. Single wraps come apart when the core is removed, making them ideal for storing extra cord on gear to keep it on hand.

The basic is a no knot wrap and is simply cord wrapped around a core in a clean spiral. It is ideal for quick wraps and has the most options for finishing.

The half cobra is a knot based wrap and offers good grip, especially with the ridge situated on flats for knives and other similar tools.

Another knot based wrap, the Helix has a ridge that spirals down the wrap. I makes a very good no-slip grip.

The crossed back is a very comfortable no knot wrap perfect for knives.

Basic Wrap	53	Half Cobra	55
Helix	59	Crossed Back	61

Single Cord

Basic Wrap

Growing up, my father would always say that you can never have too much cord. As a result, I grew up with this wrap on just about everything. It ended up on polespears, bucket handles, buckets, tent poles, broom handles, knives, tools, serving spoons, bag straps, and just about anywhere else a wrap can go.

Even now it's a major part of my life. This basic wrap, also know as whipping or lashing, is a very simple but effective way to wrap or bind anything. As a handle for a working tool it can't be beat. The continuous wrap offers good cushion and traction while keeping a surface smooth and preventing hot spots.

It's my go-to wrap for just about everything. The wrap can be twisted to loosen the cord to allow easy removal or adjustment and then twisted back to lock it in place. Because there are no knots it can be taken apart very quickly. This makes it perfect for storing lengths of cord around something like a bucket or broom handle (or anything else for that matter). This is a no-knot wrap.

1

Start by securing the end of your cord to the handle. The working end is on the lower right. Reverse the direction for a left-hand wrap.

2

Loop the working end around the back of the handle.

Wind the working end over the front of the handle and around to the back like in step 2.

The rest of the wrap is done in this way, just keep winding the working end around the handle.

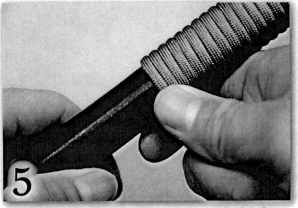

A quick way to wind the cord is to hold the working end with a light but firm grip with the hand you are wrapping towards. Grip the handle with the other hand and twist.

Continue wrapping until you've wrapped as much as you want. Keep in mind what method you are using to finish the wrap.

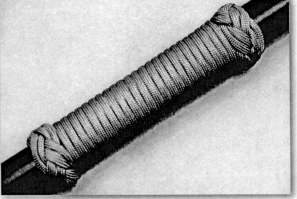

Finish up the end of the wrap. All methods of finishing will work with this wrap.

Here's the wrap all finished up. To really lock it into place, twist the wrap in the direction of the wraps. Twisting the other way will cause it to loosen.

Single Cord
Half Cobra

Effectively composed of simple loops that alternate direction, the half cobra is a versatile wrap. It gets its name because it looks just like the cobra knot with a ridge on only one side as opposed to two.

It is a simple wrap to do and works very well on knife and tool handles. The ridge offers good grip and a place for fingers to dig into and the rest of the cord offers a smooth surface that fits in the palm.

As a knot for making straps and bracelets, it is invaluable. Unlike the cobra knot, the half cobra only loops around itself. When the core it is wrapped over is removed, it simply falls apart. The cobra knot will hold together because it is a sequence of two cord knots.

This makes it great for survival bracelets and items that are wrapped mainly for carrying large amounts of cord. It can even be modified to work as a double cord wrap and is perfect for carrying large amounts of cord in a small space. A double half cobra survival bracelet can be found on page 109. This is a knot-based wrap.

1 Start with your cord secured to the handle. The working end is on the lower right.

2 Bring the working end back around and then up and over the handle until the cord is back where it started.

3

Lift up the starting end and tuck the working cord underneath it. Pull this tight to lock the wrap.

4

Now bring the cord around in the opposite direction. This will form a loop.

5

Bring the end of the cord around the back of the handle and then up through the loop. Tighten the loop to secure this knot.

6

The next knot is just like the last, just done in the opposite direction. The working cord will form a loop as it goes around the back of the handle.

7

Push the end of the cord through the loop and pull it tight.

8

Continue wrapping, alternating the direction of your turns until you reach the end.

9

Finish up the end of your wrap. Because it is a knot, burning the end works really well. The loop, over needle, and Turk's head methods all work well.

Here's the finished wrap from the top where the ridge is.

And here it is from the side. You can see that the ridge is fairly tall which can be used add a little height to one side of a wrap.

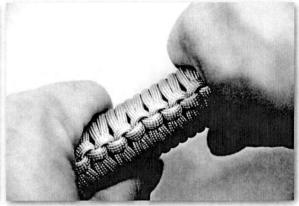

If the wrap is on a smooth surface it can slip around if twisted. To twist, grip both ends of the wrap.

Twist your hands in the opposite direction. Because the knots alternate, twisting in either direction will tighten the wrap.

Twisting gives the ridge a subtle curve around the handle which can aid in grip. It is also slightly thicker than the helix in the next section and gentler on the hands.

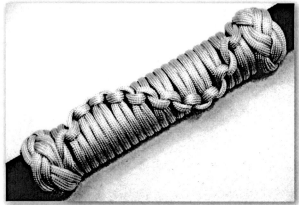

Since this wrap is tight regardless of twist direction, you can twist it in both directions for a nice decorative touch. It also can help give fingers a place to grab on tool handles.

While the half cobra wrap sticks out and is a little harder on the hands than the looped wrap, it is fairly similar in feel.

It's a good option if extra grip is only needed on one half of a handle.

It's easy to accidentally make this wrap too tight. Keeping it a little loose will make the ridge a little easier on the hands.

This is what happens when two separate helix wraps are done in opposite directions.

You end up with an x-pattern. While it's not very comfortable as a grip, it makes for a striking decorative wrap.

Single Cord

Helix

Like the half cobra, the helix is composed of simple loops over a core. The difference is that the direction of loops is constant.

As each loop is made, the resulting stack of knots naturally spirals in one direction. This gives the helix wrap its distinctive ridge.

This knot is great for handles that need a good amount of grip, especially for gloved hands. The single ridge

on this wrap digs into the hand but is still comfortable to use without gloves. This is my favorite knot for polespears.

The helix wrap is also great for adding decoration to items that are meant to hold cord. It simply falls apart if the core is removed, like the half cobra wrap. That makes it a great option for storing extra cord on gear.

The single helix also makes for a good marker when doing other wraps like the basic wrap. For example, a walking stick could have a main basic wrap with short sections of a helix wrap as length markers which can be used as a measuring tool.

Start with the end of the cord secured to the handle. The working end is to the lower right.

Bring the working end around the back of the handle and through the loop it makes. This knot is the same as the half cobra.

Pull the working end to tighten the knot. It helps at this point to pull the working end from side to side to really tighten down the knot.

Repeat the knot again. The new knot will end up next to the previous knot.

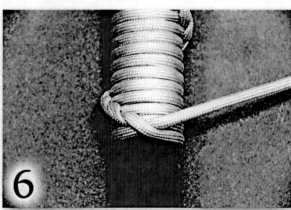

As you tie knots, the ridge formed by the knots will start spiraling in the direction you are tying.

Keep tying the knots until you reach the end.

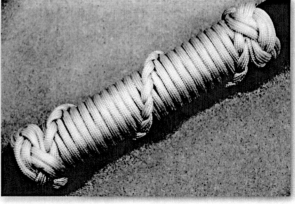

Finish the end of the wrap. Burning the ends work well as it is a knot. The loop, over needle, and Turk's head methods all work well.

Here's the wrap all finished up.

Single Cord

Crossed Back

The first time I ever did this wrap, it was by accident. While wrapping a handle with a basic wrap, I slipped and ended up crossing the cord back before continuing.

At the time, I was annoyed by the gap I had made in the wrap. Yet rather than go back and fix it, I repeated my error until I had a clean wrap that looked just like the crossed over wrap. After that, the crossed back became one of my favorites.

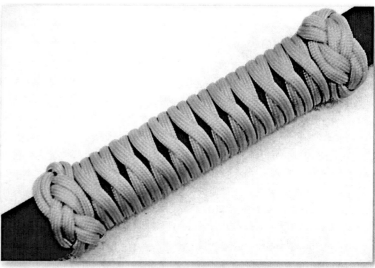

It is a simple wrap, perfect for knife handles. It offers good grip with just enough bite to keep the handle from shifting or slipping while being gentle on the hands. It is still a fairly low-profile wrap and is less likely to form hot spots.

When wrapping over round cores like walking sticks or fishing poles, keep in mind that this wrap may come apart if the cords are able to slip over each other. Stabilizing the wrap with resin can help prevent the cord slipping and unraveling. This isn't a problem for wraps over flat cores like knives. This is a no knot wrap.

1

Start with the cord secured to the handle. The working end is to the lower right.

2

Bring the working end around the back of the handle. Leave a space about a cord's width above the cord as you wrap.

Wrap the cord around the front, laying it into the space above the first wrap.

Bring the working cord back around the handle directly below the left side and a cord's width below the right.

Wrap over the front and lay the cord onto the space above on the right side. Continue around and to the back.

Flipped over, this is what the back should look like.

Continue wrapping until you reach the end.

Finish the end of the wrap. All finishing methods can work but require patience. The reverse wrap, while possible, is very tricky with this wrap.

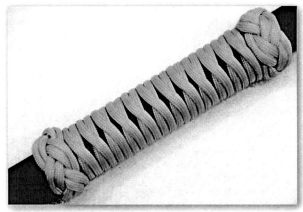

Here's the finished wrap from the front.

From the side, you can see the raised areas where the cord crosses over itself.

When applied to a flat handle or flat bar, the crossed back wrap lays fairly flat.

It's great for adding grip to knives or flat tools without creating hot spots or digging into the palm.

The wrap stays much better when done over a flat or oval handle. Round handles may need to be stabilized to prevent twist.

This handle, because it is very close to being round and the wrap has a tendency to move, is stabilized.

Because it was done over paint, care was taken to make sure the resin and solvent didn't reach the visible paint.

This was done with a light touch, just enough for the resin to soak in.

Wraps
Double Cord

Double cord wraps can be done with either a single length of cord with two working ends or two separate cords.

The crossed over is a no knot wrap that is often used on traditional Chinese and Japanese sword handles. It offers good grip and comfort.

The cobra is a popular knot-based wrap that work well for widening flat handles. It is a great wrap for straps and belts.

Like the helix, the Double helix is a knot based wrap that offers excellent grip. It really bites into the hand to reduce slipping.

The looped is a no knot wrap that is similar to the crossed over in feel with a little extra ridge on both sides.

Crossed Over	65	Cobra	67
Double Helix	72	Looped	75

Double Cord

Crossed Over

The first time I saw this wrap, it adorned the hilt of a beautiful Chinese broadsword. The grip was solid yet gentle on the hands, the raised ridges less tooth-like than the diamond wrap often seen on Japanese sword grips.

As the name suggests, this wrap is composed of two cords crossing over each other. While almost identical in appearance with the crossed back wrap, this wrap is much more stable. The two cords grip each other and keep the edges from coming up, making this a better choice for round or thicker handles.

This wrap can also be done with two or more sets of starting cord for a wrap with larger diamond spaces and an overall softer grip. A multiple cord wrap also works well with gutted Paracord, resulting in a very thin wrap that still offers good grip.

It's a no knot wrap and my personal favorite for wrapping over larger handled tools like machetes, hatchets, hammers, and shovels.

1 Start by securing your cord to the handle or by placing the center of your cord behind the handle.

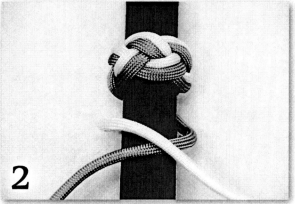

2 Bring both working ends over the front. They will cross over each other. Keep in mind which one goes over and which goes under.

3

Tighten the wrap and bring both ends around the handle.

4

Continue wrapping by repeating steps 2 and 3.

5

Once you've reached the end, finish the wrap. The Turk's head and loop methods both work really well. The over needle and knot and melt can work as well.

Here's the finished wrap from the front. If done in one color, it looks almost identical to the crossed back wrap.

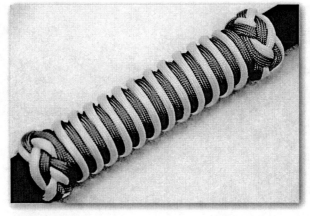

Here's the wrap from the side. The raised areas add good grip and a place for the fingers to hold on to.

Double Cord

Cobra

Also known as the Solomon bar and square knot, the cobra knot is a versatile and decorative knot. The knot itself is composed of two half knots tied around a core.

If the knots are tied in opposite directions, as in left over right and right over left, square knots are formed. The cobra knot is basically a square knot tied around a core.

If the knots are tied in the same direction, as in left

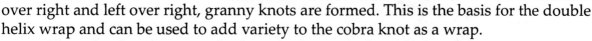

over right and left over right, granny knots are formed. This is the basis for the double helix wrap and can be used to add variety to the cobra knot as a wrap.

The cobra knot is a popular knot for lanyards, bracelets, and straps. The cobra knot survival bracelet on page 102 goes into more detail on tying the cobra knot itself for building bracelets and lanyards.

As a wrap, the cobra knot offers good grip and is great for widening handles. The two ridges do have a tendency to bite and keeping them aligned gets harder when working with larger cores. The cobra is a knot based wrap.

1 Start by securing the cord to the handle or by placing the center of the cord under the handle. We will call the light cord A and the dark cord B.

2 Start by passing the end of A behind the handle. Bring the end of B over the front of the handle.

3

Tuck the end of A up into the loop made by B. Pull the end of B through the loop made by A.

4

Pull both ends, tightening the first knot. A and B will switch sides.

5

Tying the next knot is just like the last except flipped. When tying the cobra knot A will always go around the back and B will always go around the front.

6

Once this knot is tightened, A and B switch sides again.

7

Continue tying by repeating the very first knot.

8

From here on it's all about alternating sides. It may take a little getting used to, just make sure that A stays on one side and B stays on the other.

Keep tying knots until you've reached the end of the wrap.

Finish the wrap. Melting the ends and the Turk's head work the best. The loop method works as well.

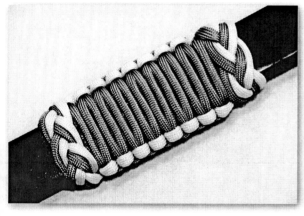

Here's the finished wrap from the front.

Here's the wrap from the side.

In this section on variations we'll play with some simple ways to make the cobra knot more visually interesting. Start with the cobra knot.

If cord A is brought over the top of the handle instead of cord B, the pattern of the wrap changes.

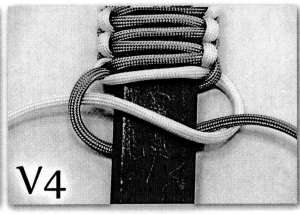

Now that the wrap is reversed, there are a couple ways to go. Bringing B back to the front would start a double helix wrap.

By keeping A over the front of the handle, the wrap will continue on slightly to one side.

A sort of delayed helix can be achieved by doing an odd number of knots in one direction and then switching.

Switching back to B over the front on an even number will bring the wrap back to its previous position.

The resulting knot continues the previous pattern, leaving only one patch of reversed coloration.

This is sometimes called the heart knot or the heart bar because the two inner bars resemble a heart shape. This especially evident on narrower wraps.

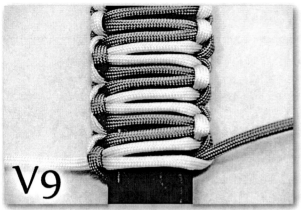

V9

If the direction is switched back and forth, you end up with alternating colored hearts. The sides of the wrap also gain a more staggered appearance.

V10

Go back to step V3 where the wrap had just been reversed.

V11

Bringing B back to the front of the handle starts a double helix wrap.

V12

You can already see the wrap beginning to twist around the handle.

V13

Continue wrapping, alternating between A and B being over the front of the handle.

V14

As this double helix wrap is continued, the cord will spiral around the handle. It's a good way to add some depth or grip to a flat bar.

Double Cord

Double Helix

Like the cobra knot, the double helix is composed of half knots tied around a core. The half knots in this wrap are all tied in the same direction, forming a stack of granny knots. This knot tends to jam and lock up when tightened.

This results in a wrap that is very secure and stable on its own. Like the helix, it is great for handles that need to lock in the hand. The very aggressive ridges bite into gloved hands well. It's a great wrap for flashlights and makes a great fob for keys due to its tight spiral shape. A great example of a double helix key fob can be found on page 137.

When I first learned this wrap, I started calling it the DNA wrap because of its resemblance to stylized renderings of DNA. It's a great way to add decoration and character and can be used as a stopper to separate other wraps or add extra grip in certain areas of a wrap.

This knot based wrap will also work on flat cores as shown on page 71.

1

Start by securing the cord to the handle. This wrap works well with a simple two cord start. The light cord is A and the dark cord is B.

2

Depending on which way you want the wrap to spiral, cross the working ends one over the other. A on top will spiral to the right, B on top will spiral to the left.

3

Since we're wrapping to the right, bring the end of A under the loop made by B.

4

Tighten the knot. If you are doing this knot on a flat bar, treat it like the start of a cobra knot.

5

Bring A around the back of the handle and then pass B under the end of A and then into the loop A makes.

6

Pull the ends tight and straight to the sides. This will allow the two crossed areas of the knot to sit exactly opposite of each other.

7

Repeat step 5 with the cords swapped. Bring A around the back of the handle and then pass A under the end of B and then into the loop B makes.

8

Pull the working ends to tighten the knot. You can already start to see the twist.

Continue tying knots by repeating steps 5 to 8 until you've reached the end.

Once you've reached the end, finish the wrap. Melting the ends and the Turk's head work the best. The loop method works as well.

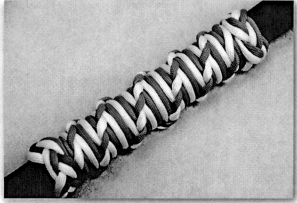

Here's the finished double helix wrap.

A twist in the direction of the knots gives you a tighter spiral. Tightening the knots like this offers a better grip on the handle plus a better grip in the hand.

The wrap on the left is often called a diamond wrap or sword wrap for its use on Japanese and Chinese swords.

It is essentially the crossed over wrap on the right with a few twists in the cord added.

You can find this wrap on page 87.

Double Cord
Looped

The first time I saw this wrap was during college when a friend needed his cord-handled knife re-wrapped. Since then this wrap has exploded in popularity among both custom knifemakers and production knife and tool companies.

What is nice about this wrap is that it has a large ridge much like knot based wraps, but the ridge is less defined and ends up being softer in the hand. This makes for a wrap with good grip while still comfortable for prolonged use.

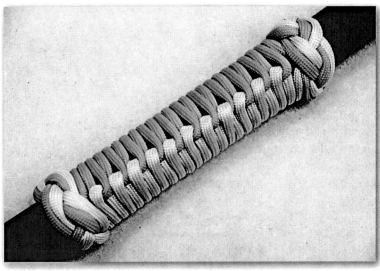

While it does work on round cores and larger handles, this wrap excels when used on thin cores. It is well suited for knives with full tangs and no handle slabs. The extra body of this wrap gives a nice full grip. This is a good wrap for increasing the handle size of knives that may be too thin for your grip.

While it is a more comfortable wrap than the knot based wraps, it still is not recommended for tools that will be under a lot of heavy or repeated use like hammers, axes, machetes, or chopping knives.

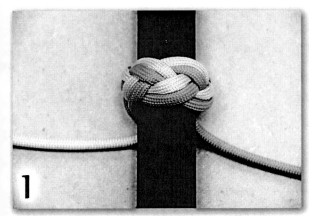

1

Start by securing your cord to the handle or by placing the center of your cord behind the handle.

2

Cross one cord over the other. For a uniform wrap, make sure the same top cord stays on the top.

Twist the cords so that each cord is essentially hooked on to the other.

Pull the working ends tight. Much like the crossed over wraps, this wrap does not lock itself.

Turn the handle over. Cross the cords over each other.

Twist the cords so that they are hooked on each other and then tighten.

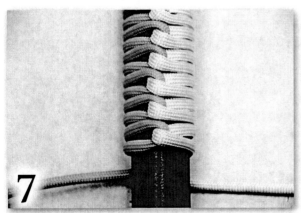

Continue wrapping until you reach the end of your handle or length of wrap.

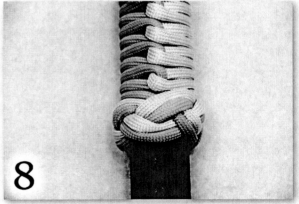

Once you've reached the end, finish the wrap. The Turk's head and loop methods both work really well. The over needle and knot and melt can work as well.

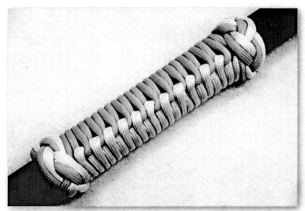

Here's the finished wrap from the front.

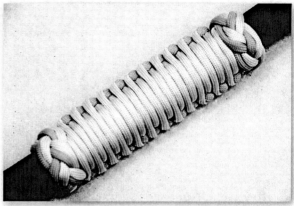

Here's the finished wrap from the side. You can see the raised ridge on the front and back.

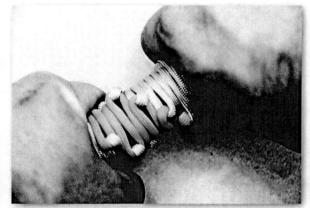

Much like the half cobra and cobra wraps, this wrap can be twisted to form a loose spiral. This is one way to tighten down the wrap.

Like the helix and double helix, this twist offers a good grip on handles and gives places for the fingers to dig into.

The looped wrap is a very popular wrap for knives, flat prybars, and any other tool that needs a very secure grip.

Many knife companies and custom makers offer knives with this style of wrap, like the neck knife pictured here.

Chapter Four
Wrap Alongs

Now that we have a basic idea of how to perform the wraps in this book, it's time to put them together with other techniques to make complete and finished wraps. In this chapter, we will take a couple basic wraps and introduce some new variations to wrapping and finishing.

Basically I will show you how I would take on some projects, how to figure out where to start and finish, as well as some different techniques to change the overall feel of some wraps. This way you can wrap along with me and put the different wraps and methods into practice.

Since the last chapter mainly dealt with wrapping over a round core or handle, this chapter mainly deals wraps that work well with knives and flat tools.

Wrap Alongs

Crossed Over - Long Knife

In this wrap along, we'll be turning a knife blank cut from an old sword into a general purpose chopping knife. Here are some of the more detailed sections that will help you with your own projects.

The first thing we'll do is an under wrap, which is one way to add some thickness and width to a knife tang before wrapping.

Next is the Turk's head knot. Since wrapping over a flat handle is slightly different than a round bar, we'll go step by step to build the guard on this knife.

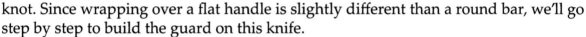

Once the handle is wrapped with a crossed over wrap, we'll finish with another Turk's head knot. After that the final step is to stabilize the Paracord with resin to make the wrap permanent. This is one of my favorite methods as it requires no vacuum equipment or messy two part resins. Keep in mind that this should be done outdoors or in a very well ventilated area.

Well, let's get wrapping. Here we go!

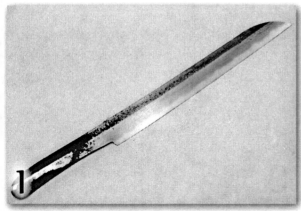

The knife we'll be wrapping has a handle with some contour to it.

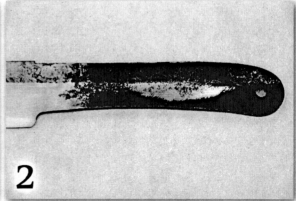

The handle is bare and rather rough. An under-wrap will cover the steel beneath and give extra body to the handle.

3

Lay the end of the cord over the handle. There should be about 2-3 inches of overhang that will become the standing end.

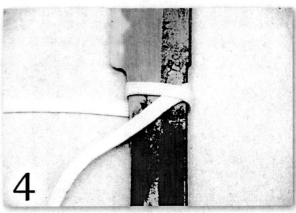

4

Fold the short standing end down and begin wrapping the working end around it and the handle.

5

Keep wrapping until the standing end is secured. This is the wrap over method.

6

Wrap until 2-3 inches from the end of where the main wrap will end.

7

Lay the working end along the handle. The end should be near the top and the bottom forms a big loop.

8

Wrap the rest of the handle with the loop made by the working cord. The working end will be covered by the wrap.

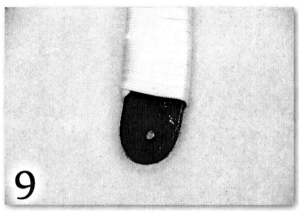

Pull the working end to tighten and finish the wrap. This is a modified version of the reverse wrap.

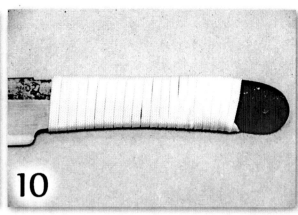

Here's the finished under-wrap. This was done with gutted cord. For a thicker handle, use full cord.

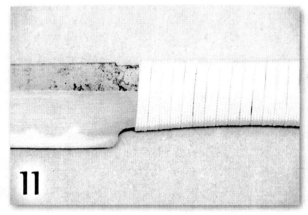

Next we'll place a Turk's head knot to serve as a finger guard and to separate blade from handle.

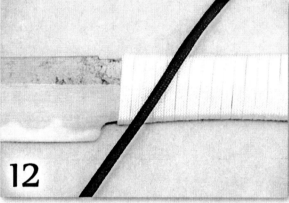

Start by placing your cord over the handle. The working end is to the right. I suggest using a longer cord to tie this knot as the excess can be pulled through and saved later.

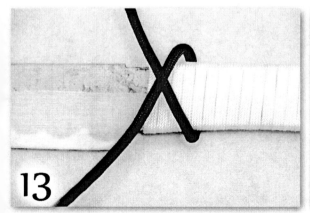

Bring the working end around the back of the handle and then cross it over itself.

Pass the working end over the back of the handle. Then bring the working end up between the standing end and the first loop, then cross over the first loop.

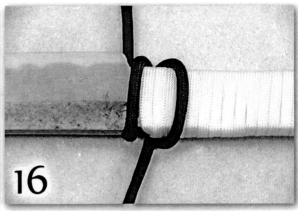

Pass the working end under the standing end. It should look like this with the working end pointing up and the standing end pointing down.

Flip the handle over. The working end should now be pointing down and the standing end should be pointing up.

Take the left loop and pull it over the right loop. Be sure to only overlap them slightly and not completely pull the left loop over the right.

Push the working end under the bottom loop and then pull it all the way through.

Push the working end under the top portion of the right loop and then pull it all the way through.

Flip the handle over. At this point, if the handle is larger and needs more body, repeat steps 6-11 to add another set of woven loops.

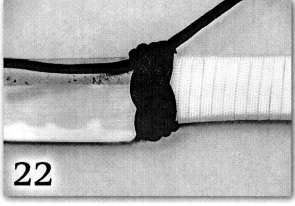

To finish up the first layer of the knot, start by pushing the working end under the same loop the standing end is under.

Follow the first pass to double up the knot.

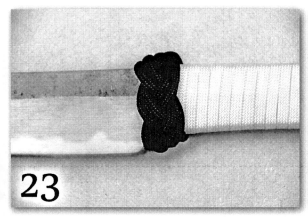

Once the knot is tightened, trim and secure the loose ends.

Place the handle over the center of the main cord. I'm using gutted cord for a thinner wrap.

Bring both working ends over the front. They will cross over each other. Keep in mind which one goes over and which goes under.

Flip the handle over and cross the cords over each other again.

For a consistent wrap, make sure the top cord is always on top.

Continue until the end of the under-wrap.

Tie the two ends together. This will keep the wrap in place temporarily.

Tie a Turk's head knot to finish the end of the wrap.

While the knot is still loose, untie the temporary knot and pass both cords underneath the Turk's head knot.

Tighten the knot, pull all the loose ends tight, and then trim them.

33 Here's the finished wrap. If you plan on stabilizing the handle, be sure to make any adjustments now before the cord is fused together.

34 In order to make the wrap more permanent, we'll be stabilizing it with resin. While there are many ways to do this, I prefer using wood hardener or stabilizer.

High Performance
Wood Hardener
• Penetrates deep into wood
• Reinforces soft wood fibers

35 Keep in mind that there are solvents involved, so be sure to wear lung and eye protection as well as solvent-resistant gloves. Work in a well-ventilated area.

36 With a natural bristle brush, begin dabbing the wood stabilizer onto the paracord. It will quickly soak into the material.

37 Keep applying the stabilizer in light coats until the paracord appears wet and won't absorb any more.

38 Keep applying stabilizer until the whole wrap is soaked through.

Here's the finished handle. Allow the wrap to dry in a well-ventilated area for at least a day. If needed, apply another light coat. Do not over-apply as the wrap will end up looking like plastic. Over the next few days the resin will set and the finish will fully-cure.

Here's the finished knife. This style of wrap is one of my favorites for finishing smaller neck knives and larger chopping knives. It offers a good grip, yet does not bite into the hand or create hot-spots.

The crossed over wrap works really well for any tool that needs a little extra grip.

Many tools have checkered or rough handles to aid in grip, but often can cause blisters with prolonged use.

A smooth but grippy wrap like the crossed back or crossed over wrap is a great way to increase comfort.

Wrap Alongs
Diamond Wrap - Tanto

I have always had a fascination with knives and swords. Like many, I admire the Japanese katana and its simple beauty.

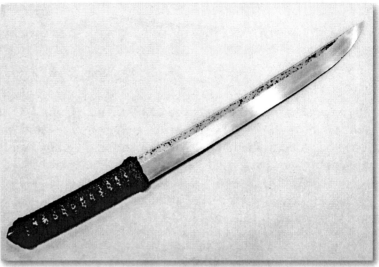

The wrap in this section is a simplified version of a wrap found on many antique swords. Today this style of wrap has become iconic; synonymous with Samurai and the katana itself.

It is sometimes called the diamond wrap and forms a diamond pattern that shows off the under-wrap or core beneath. The grip it offers is superb, each ridge formed by the folded cord acting like a tooth that keeps the grip in your hand. It makes a great wrap for tools or knives that may become wet or will be used with gloved hands.

This particular knife is actually the tip portion of a broken sword, given new life. We will go over one way to put skin or other material that will show through the diamond gaps in the wrap, a technique used on many Asiatic knife and sword handles. Because the cords needs to be folded, this only works with gutted cord.

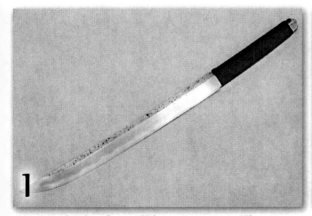

Here's the knife we'll be wrapping. The tang was simple and flat, basically the same width and thickness of the blade. The handle is already under-wrapped and stabilized.

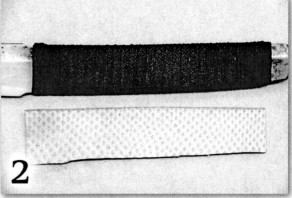

Cut two panels of leather/skin that will show through the diamond wrap. Each should be just big enough to cover one side of the handle.

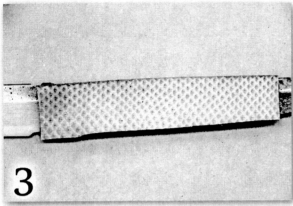

3

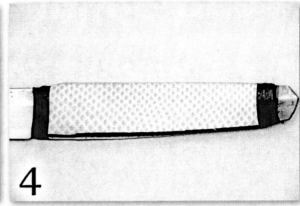

4

Place the skin or leather over the handle. The skin can be held down by the wrap only, or it can be glued to the handle with contact cement.

Cut a 1/4" strip of electrical tape or other thin tape and tape the ends of both slabs down tot he handle. These will hold everything in place.

5

6

Loosely tie a Turk's head knot over the top of the wrap. The thickness of two or three passes also serves as an integral guard.

Fold the main cord in the center and tuck it under the Turk's head wrap. Pull about an inch of the center through.

7

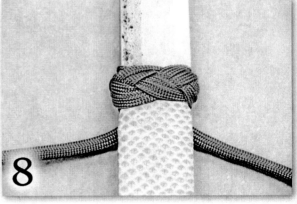

8

Tighten the Turk's head wrap, securing the main cord underneath.

Flip the handle over to begin the diamond wrap.

Fold the left cord over the front of the handle.

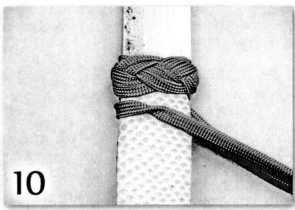

Pull the cord tight and give it an inward twist where it rests at the center of the handle.

Twist the cord again. Make sure the cord is actually folded and not just twisted to keep the wrap from looking sloppy.

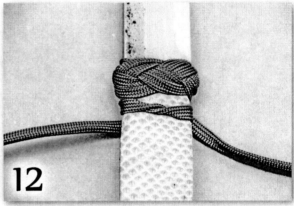

Pull the cord tight around the back of the handle. The first half of the wrap should look like this.

Fold the right cord over the front of the handle.

Give the cord an inward twist so that it lays over the twist in the other cord.

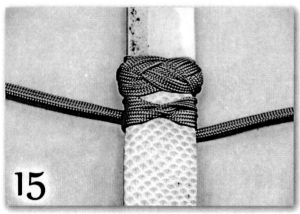

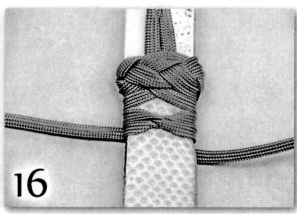

Twist the cord again and the two cords should lock together at the area of the twist on the cord is pulled tight.

Flip the handle over and repeat steps 8-15 to finish another section of wrap.

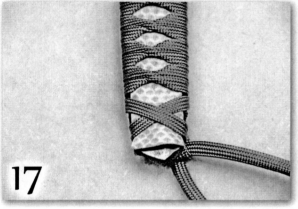

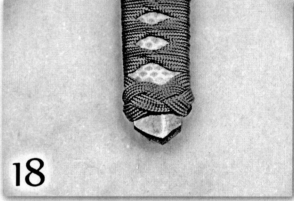

Continue wrapping until the end. To finish the end, do a single crossed over wrap and tie off the end to keep everything tight.

Tie a Turk's head knot over the crossed over wrap and tighten it down. The Turk's head will hold the ends securely. Trim all loose ends.

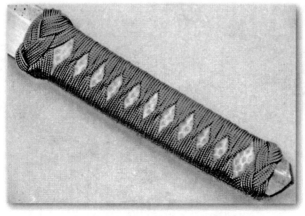

Here's the finished handle wrap before stabilizing with resin.

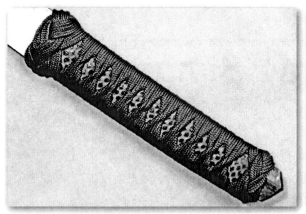
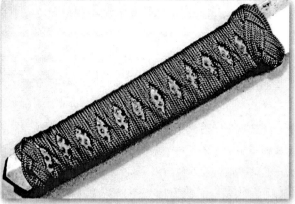

After stabilizing with resin, notice the darkening of the wrap and skin. Keep that in mind when planning to stabilize lighter colors.

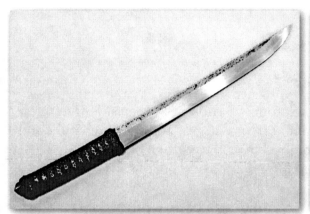

The finished wrap from both sides. This style of wrap really compliments the look of Asiatic-styled knives as well as most knives that lack defined handles. It offers superb grip but does have a tendency to bite into the hand, making it a good option for gloved hands.

The first two knives from this chapter and the small knife in the right corner were actually cut from an old Japanese sword that had been broken during World War II.

Paracord wrapping is a great way to turn a broken or bare-tanged blade into a functional and comfortable knife with little to no metal work.

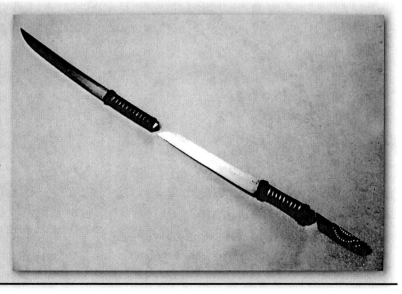

Wrap Alongs
Between Bars - Slingshot

This next wrap-along is a variation on the basic wrap. I call it the between bars or figure eight wrap because of the way the cord weaves between the two bars of the handle.

I'm wrapping a bent-rod slingshot, taking advantage of the two aluminum rods that makes up the handle. This wrap also works well for knives and tools with split or skeletonized handles.

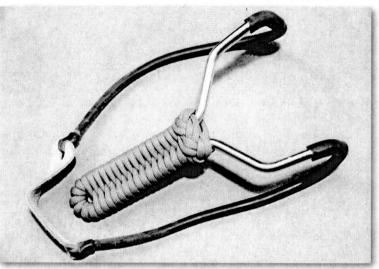

The grip is excellent, especially for skeletonized knives. The center of the wrap is slightly concave, giving the fingers a place to dig in without adding much bulk and keeping a slim profile. This is also a good method for binding two or more sticks or rods together. I'll sometimes use it for making tent poles or beams out of smaller saplings.

The end of the slingshot is finished by continuing a basic wrap around the bent rod. This is a simple way to finish and add cushion to a ring or rounded end of a skeletonized handle.

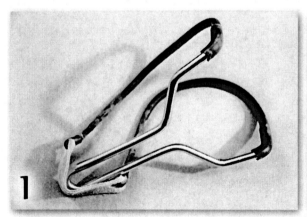

1 Here's the slingshot frame we'll be wrapping. This is a nice wrap for any type of split frame or for joining two bars together.

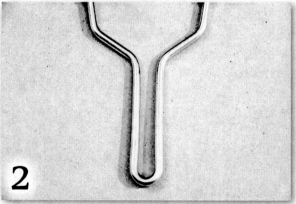

2 Start by laying out the handle or bars to be wrapped.

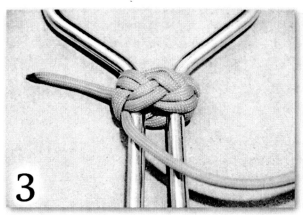

3

Start by securing the cord to the top of the handle to be wrapped. Here I am using a Turk's head over both bars. The cord can also be connected to only one side.

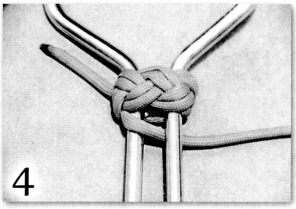

4

Take the working end and pass it in between the two bars to the back.

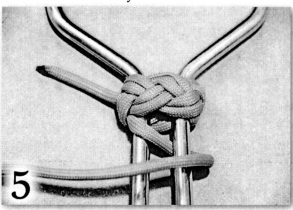

5

Pull the cord around to the front of the handle.

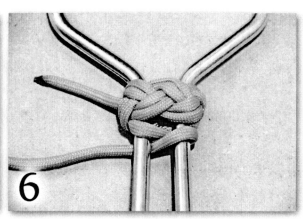

6

Pass the cord back through the center between the two bars.

7

Bring the cord around to the front again and follow up by passing it through the center again.

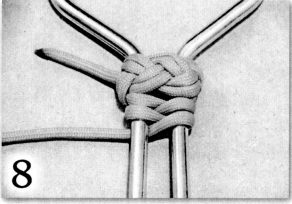

8

The wrap simply winds around the two bars in a figure-eight fashion.

9

After every four or five passes, push the wraps up to tighten the pattern and remove any gaps. It's also a good idea to tighten the wrap as you go.

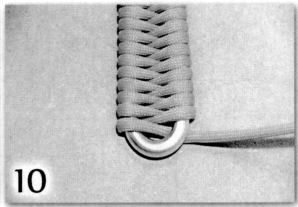

10

Continue wrapping to the end. The end can be finished with a Turk's head or any other method. We will be finishing by looping around the bottom.

11

Push the working end through the loop or ring at the bottom.

12

Pull the working end tight and pass it through the ring or loop again.

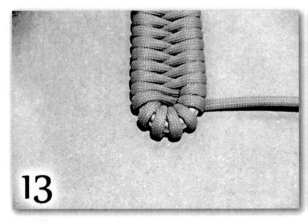

13

Continue wrapping until the cord on the inside edge is tightly packed.

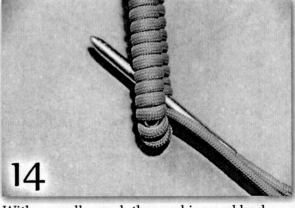

14

With a needle, push the working end back through the main wraps. Start at the last full wrap and exit at least two wraps up. This will ensure a secure wrap.

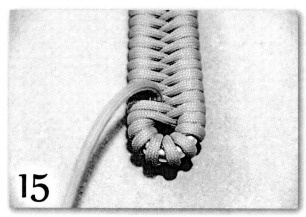

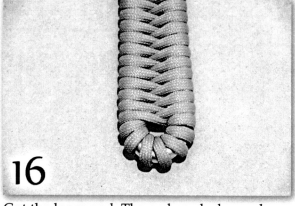

Here you can see the end tucked through the last two wraps.

Cut the loose end. The end can be burned and fused to the surface of the wrap. I prefer to hide the loose end in the wrap and apply a drop of superglue to secure it.

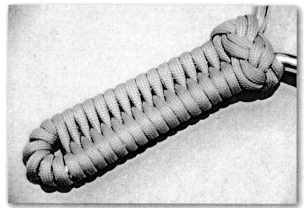

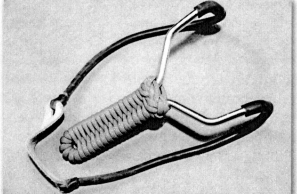

Here's the finished handle.

This wrap works really well for adding grip while not adding much thickness to a handle. It works great on bent-rod fish nets and other tools with split or wire handles.

The handle on the right was stabilized and the loose ends were hidden within the wrap while the handle on the left is not stabilized and the loose ends are melted.

Sometimes it can be better to keep a handle unstabilized as the cord stays soft and has a bit of cushion to it. It all depends on what the wrap is used for.

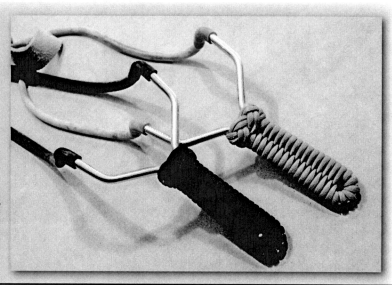

Wrap Alongs

Crossed Back - Thrower

When I was a boy, my father would teach me to use polespears, shoot bows, and throw knives among other things. This knife was a gift for my eighth birthday, a large and well-balanced thrower with a simple but elegant paracord wrap. My old companion has long since lost its handle wrap and deserves a new one.

The wrap here is a crossed back wrap, though any wrap can be done. The real power of this simple wrap is the way it is started and finished. It makes use of a hole at the top and bottom of the handle to be wrapped where an overhand knot is used as a stopper. Many knives have pin holes and the ones that don't have them usually have a thong or lanyard hole which can be used to finish the wrap.

This wrap along is pretty straightforward, the main point being starting and finishing the wrap with a knot that creates a stopper to hold the wrap in place. Most times two cords can be used in order to do double cord wraps or two-color wraps. If the loose ends are left an inch or two long after the knots, the wrap can be re-tied.

1

Here's the throwing knife we'll be putting a new wrap on. It has a hole near the top of the handle and another near the bottom, which are common places for pin holes.

2

We'll start the wrap at the top of the handle, though it can be started at the bottom as well.

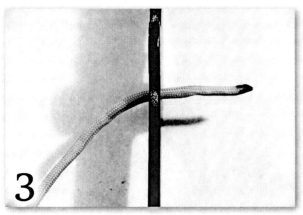

Push the end of your cord through the pin hole. The end of your cord may have to be heated and rolled to a point in order to fit.

Pull the loose end through until you have enough cord to tie an overhand knot.

Tie an overhand knot and pull it tight from both sides. Make sure the knot is secure by pulling hard from the back side.

Once the knot is secure, trim and burn the end. The loose ends can be left an inch or two long to allow the wrap to be re-tied if removed.

Begin your wrap of choice. I'm using the crossed back wrap.

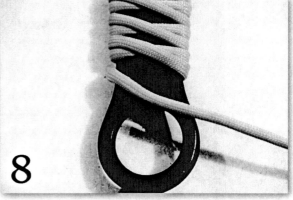

Continue wrapping until the end.

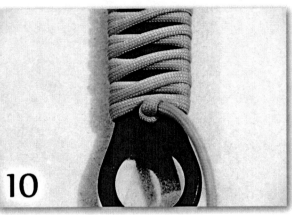

Push the working end through the bottom pin hole.

Flip the handle over and tie an overhand knot.

Trim and melt the end of the knot and the wrap is finished!

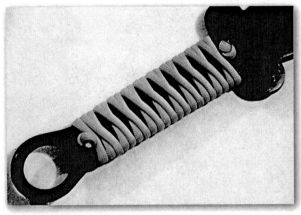

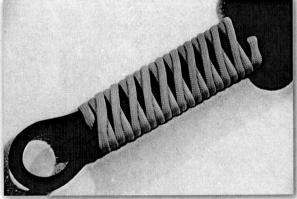

The finished wrap from the front and back. This method works very well for securing base or under-wraps.

Here's the whole knife from the front and back. Another way to change the feel of this technique is to have one knot on one side and one on the other.

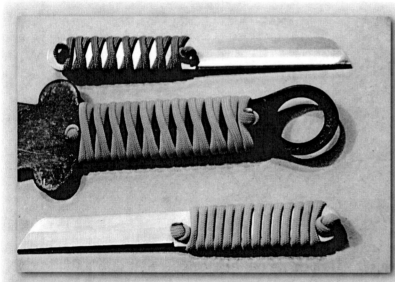

Here are some smaller utility knives with paracord handles that use the stopper knots.

While this method works best for single cord wraps, it can also be used for double cord wraps.

A good way to do this is to have a stopper knot on each side of the handle. This evens the handle out and locks the knots in place.

Here are the three knives from the wrap-alongs.

From a distance, the crossed back, crossed over, and diamond wrap all look similar.

While they are done differently, these three wraps all follow the same basic idea.

Chapter Five

Bracelets and Straps

This chapter is all about making practical and decorative items using only Paracord. By using the wraps and knots in the previous chapters combined with some new ones, many different projects can be created.

Survival bracelets are a great way to carry a little bit of cord wherever you go. In this section, we'll build a few basic styles that look good and can be taken apart quickly. These can also be modified with some extra hardware and a little bit of imagination to make watch bands, hair ties, pet collars, and more.

In the second section we will go over making straps, keychains, fobs, pulls and tags. Making small projects is also a great way to practice knotting, tying, and finishing. They can help you keep track of and identify important things like your keys, luggage, bags, and more. These make great gifts for family, friends, and even to sell to help fund your hobby.

Bracelets and Straps
Survival Bracelets

Even though I grew up with Paracord and simple wraps, it wasn't until college that I discovered the survival bracelet.

The idea is simple, wear a bracelet made of a good length of Paracord (anywhere from 6 to 20 feet) and have it on you everywhere you go. If you are ever in a situation where the cord becomes necessary, simply pull the bracelet apart and you have your cord.

There are many different styles and variations on the survival bracelet, these are just a few simple ones that don't require any special hardware.

Survival Bracelets

Cobra

My first introduction to the cobra survival bracelet was back in college. At the time, I knew it in the form of a combat bracelet. I had grown up with paracord but had never before thought of wearing it as a way to carry cord.

The cobra bracelet has become synonymous with the survival bracelet. While the cobra is not as easy to take apart as other knots, it still allows a large amount of cord to be packed into a small space.

While there are many ways to build a cobra knot survival bracelet, this method is one of the most simple to make and deploy. The core is separate and easily removed to allow the knots to collapse and open up for use. The core itself uses a loop and knot to secure the bracelet, though a button or other toggle at the end would work as well.

With a little modification this bracelet can be changed to use buckles, clips or other hardware instead of the loop and knot. This method of tying a cobra knot can also be used to cover belts and add body to ropes or straps.

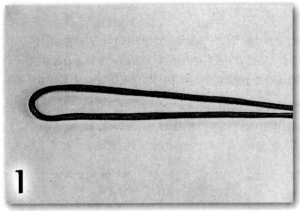

1 Measure around your wrist. Cut a length of cord 3 times that length. Fold the length of cord in half.
This will become the bracelet core.

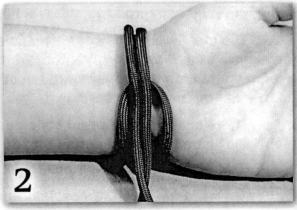

2 Place the looped end on your wrist and bring the other two ends around your wrist until they overlap the loop.

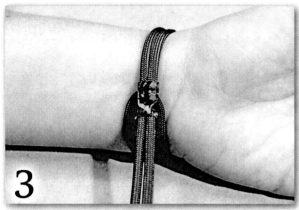

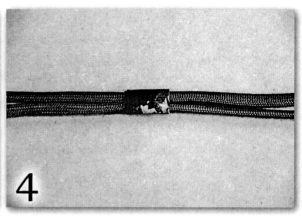

With a 3/4 inch wide strip of tape, mark the cords where they touch the loop. This will give the stopper knot some space to allow for thickness changes.

Lay the bracelet core down with the loop to the left and the loose ends to the right.

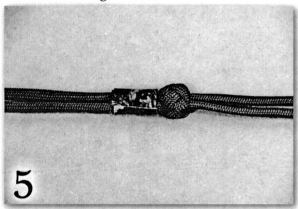

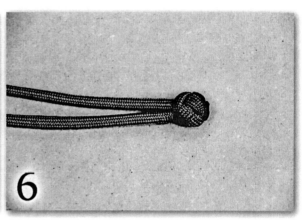

Tie an overhand or lanyard knot with the loose ends, using the tape as a guide.

Remove the tape and finish the end of the knot.

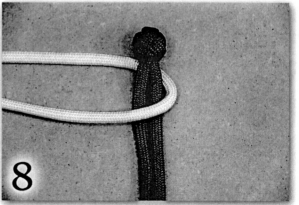

The cobra knot will use about 9.5-10 inches of cord per inch of bracelet plus around an extra foot for finishing. Place the center of this length under the bracelet core.

Start by tying an overhand knot to hold the end secure. Fold the right cord over the core of the bracelet.

If you want to skip this, start with step 12.

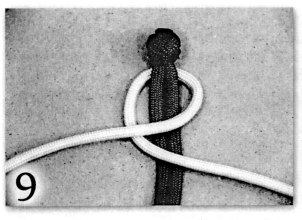

Bring the left cord underneath the right cord and over the core.

Tuck the left cord into the loop formed by the right cord.

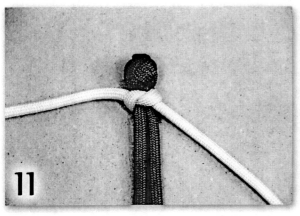

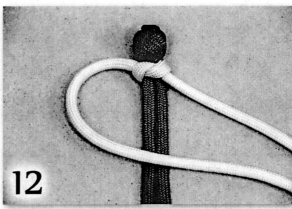

Pull the ends to tighten the overhand knot. Make sure there is a little bit of space under the stopper knot.

If starting from here, the cord will lie underneath the core.
Fold the left cord over the core.

Bring the left cord underneath the right cord.

Tuck the right cord around the back of the core and then push it through the loop formed by the left cord.

Pull the ends to tighten up the first cobra knot.

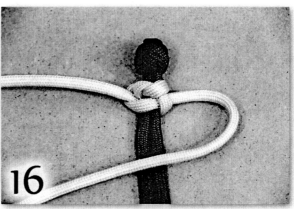

The next knot in the sequence will be opposite of the first.
Fold the right cord over the core.

Bring the left cord under the core.
Next, tuck both ends through the loops like in the picture above.

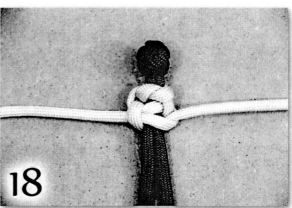

Tighten the ends to finish the second cobra knot.

The third knot is just like the first.
Fold the left cord over the core.

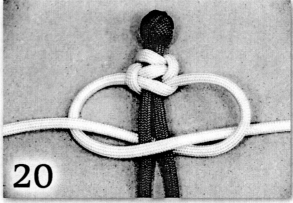

Bring the right cord under the core.
Next, tuck both ends through the loops like in the picture above.

Tighten the ends to finish up the third knot.

Here's the fourth knot, just like the second. Keep alternating sides to continue the pattern.

Here's the fifth knot, just like the first and third knots.

Continue knotting until you've reached the end of the bracelet. The resulting loop should be just large enough to fit the stopper knot, but small enough to hold it in place.

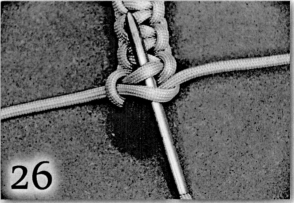

The ends can be trimmed and melted, but for a cleaner finish they can be tucked under. To do this, loosen up the last knot slightly.

Using a lacing needle or the stiffened end of the cord on the side with bars like in the picture above, tuck the end of the cord into the knot.

Pull the end through but do not tighten it yet.

Flip the bracelet over and repeat step 26 by tucking the end of the cord under and into the knot.

Pull the end through the knot.

Tighten the knot by pulling the slack out of it using the loops you left slightly loose.

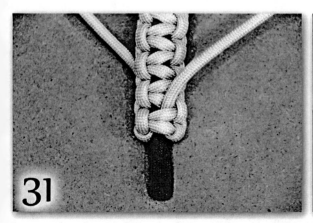

Pull the loose ends to secure the cords inside the cobra knot.

A drop of superglue where the cord comes out from inside the cobra knot will help keep it secure.

With a sharp knife, trim the loose end. For extra security, the loose end can be trimmed and then melted before being pushed gently into the knot to hide it.

Here's the finished end. This method is much cleaner than simply melting the ends, though both are equally secure.

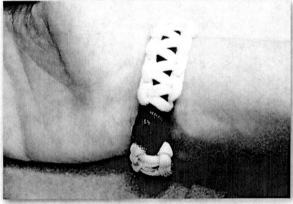

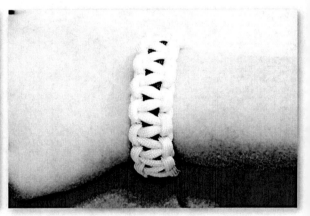

To wear the bracelet, push the knot through the end loop. The loop size can be adjusted by pushing the knots together or pulling them apart slightly.

Here's the bracelet from the top. You can see the core easily, which can give good contrast without using spliced cord.

Here's the finished cobra bracelet.
For extra cord capacity, an extra layer of knots can be applied over the first. This is called the king cobra weave and is on page 141.
If doing a king cobra, make the core about an inch longer than normal.

Survival Bracelets

Double Half Cobra

When I began making survival bracelets, deploying cord quickly was always a problem. Because both working ends of a cobra knot loop around each other, the knots stay in place fairly well even with the core removed. This makes taking the bracelet apart time consuming.

This bracelet uses two half cobra knots to give the general look of a cobra knot in the end. There are two internal bars per loop as opposed to the cobra's one which results in a much tighter knot that does not show the core color very well. Another plus is that it packs more cord for the same finished length.

The main difference comes when deploying the cord. Since both working ends make their own knots independent of the other, the whole thing simply comes apart if the core is removed. This makes taking the bracelet apart a breeze.

The double half cobra is also a great wrap for handles where the core needs to be hidden.

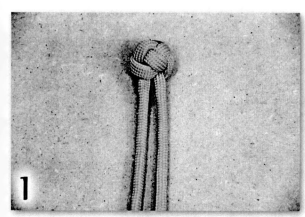

Start out by making the core loop from pages 102 and 103.

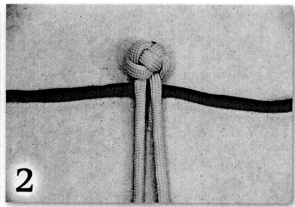

Place the center of your cord underneath the stopper knot of the core. This knot will use about 14 inches of cord per inch of bracelet plus around an extra foot for finishing.

Choose the side you want to start the wrap with and fold it behind the core. It will leave a small loop.

Loop the working end over the core.

Pass the working end through the loop made by the first pass underneath the core.

Pull the working end tight to create the first half cobra knot.

Take the other working end and pass it under the core. This will form a loop between the cord and core.

Bring the working end back over the front of the core.

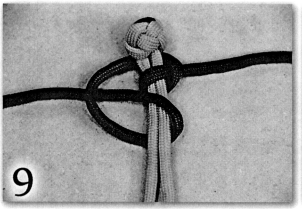

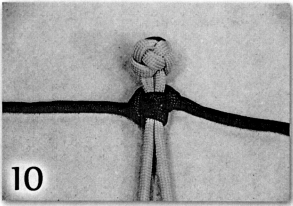

Tuck the working end underneath the loop made by the cord and core.

Tighten to form the second half cobra knot.

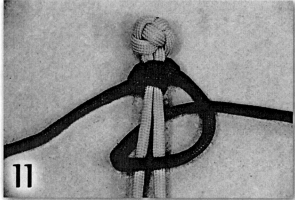

Switch over to the first cord. Prepare to make another half-cobra knot, except pass the cord over the core and then under as opposed to the under-over of previous steps.

Pull the working end through the loop and tighten to form the third half cobra knot.

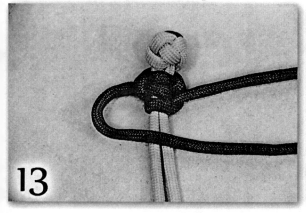

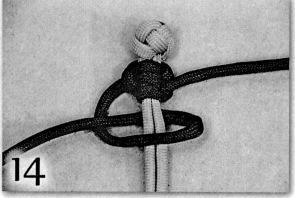

Just like in step 11, take the second cord and fold it over the core to create a loop between cord and core.

Loop the working end under the core and through the starting loop.

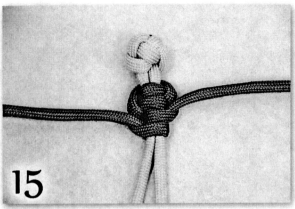

Pull the loose end tight to finish the fourth knot.

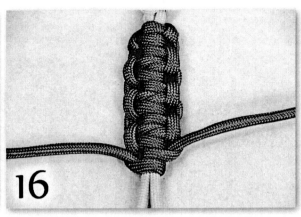

Repeat steps 3-15 and continue tying knots. Make sure to alternate between over-under and under-over.

Continue tying knots to the end. The loop should be just large enough for the stopper knot to fit.

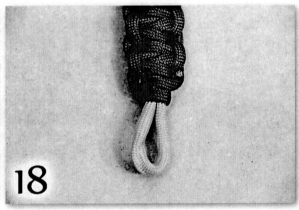

Finish the ends. Melting works really well, though the ends can be tucked in just like the cobra knot bracelet on pages 106-108.

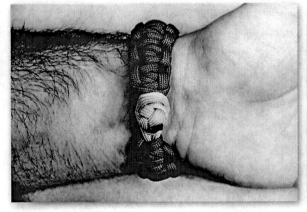

Here's the finished bracelet from the bottom. The stopper knot should fit snugly in the end loop.

Here's the finished bracelet from the top. Notice the doubled core as compared to a cobra knot bracelet.

While it can be tricky to get a hang of, this bracelet is very easy to take apart. It also holds more cord than a comparable cobra knot bracelet.

The cobra and double half cobra may look similar in solid colors, but the way they are put together is very different.

When using two colors, the cobra knot will display one color in the bars and the other color in the loops.

The double half cobra will be half one color and half the other.

Any survival bracelet can be made with buckles or clips at the ends instead of having a knot/loop closure.

Start by looping the core or starting line through one side of the buckle. Once the bracelet is finished, tuck the working end through the other side of the buckle and tuck under the knots.

Here is a cobra and a double chain sinnet.

Survival Bracelets

Double Chain Sinnet

This bracelet and its variants are my favorites when I need cord in a hurry. They are also known as caterpillar and centipede bracelets.

Unlike the cobra and half cobra which are built over a core, the chain sinnet creates its own core so to speak. This means the entire bracelet is made of one length of cord.

Like the name suggests, this bracelet uses two chain sinnets looped into each other. The two chain sinnets give the bracelet more body and keep both working ends on one side. Deploying the bracelet is much easier with both ends on one side.

This bracelet is unique in that it can be made to length as you go, as opposed to the cobra that requires a core of the right length before starting. The double chain sinnet also makes a great base for keychains, lanyards, and long straps. Even a long belt or sling can be unraveled in seconds.

Because of how simple these are to put together and unravel, I like to keep an inch or two of cord after the knot. This way the bracelet can be put together after use.

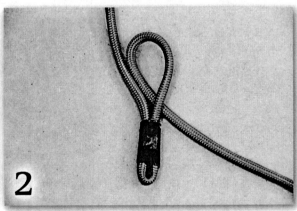

This knot will use about 9 inches of cord per inch of bracelet plus around an extra foot for finishing. Tie or tape off about 3/4" on the end to make your loop.

Take the right cord and make a loop. The loop should go under and away from the rest of the cord.

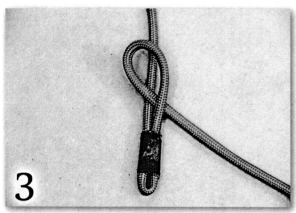

Bring the loop over the left cord in preparation for the next step.

Reach into the right loop and pull the left cord through. This will form a loop inside of the first loop. Make sure this loop comes up from under.

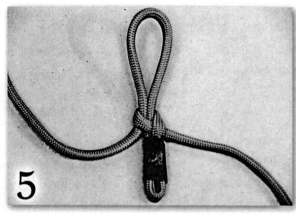

Pull the working end of the right cord, locking the loop down into a slip knot. This knot will hold everything together.

Push the right cord into the left loop. Make sure the cord goes in from the front for the rest of the knots.

Pull the working end of the left side to tighten the knot.

Pull the loop tight to clean up the knot.

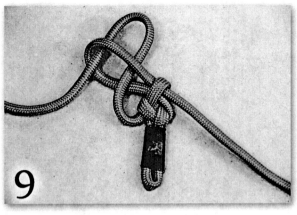

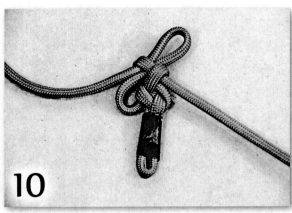

Push the left cord into the right loop from the front.

Pull the working end of the right cord to tighten the knot and form a loop.

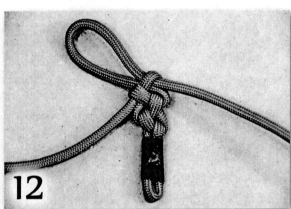

Pull the loop tight to clean up the knot.

From here repeat the steps starting from 6.

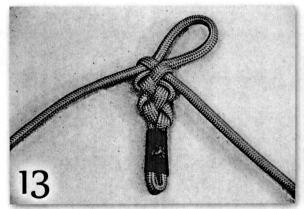

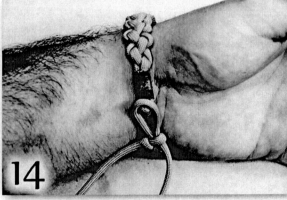

Keep building up the bracelet until it's the length you want.

When the bracelet is just long enough that a one inch loop will overlap the starting loop it's time to finish the bracelet up.

This is the last loop. The loop may be to the right or left, it doesn't matter.

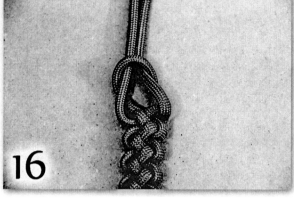

Pass both working ends through the loop.

Pull the ends, locking the cord in place. This knot shouldn't be too tight. That way it can be easily undone later on.

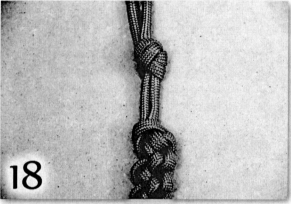

Tie an overhand or similar knot to finish the bracelet. I prefer an overhand knot for ease of removal. A lanyard knot would be a more attractive and permanent option.

Here's the bracelet finished. If you want to be able to re-tie the bracelet if it is unraveled, trim the loose ends about one to two inches from the knot.

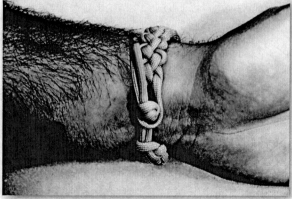

Test the fit of the bracelet out. Here it is from the bottom. If the end loop is too large or small, it can be adjusted by slowly working slack to or away from the end.

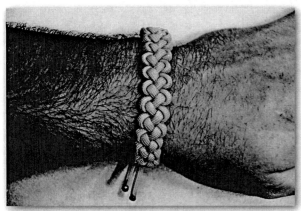

Here's the finished bracelet from the top.

Once you get a hang of starting the knot out, these bracelets are very easy to make. Putting one together can take as little as a few minutes.

While it is very easy to put together and take apart, it is a very low-capacity bracelet for holding cord. By adding additional loops, the bracelet can carry more cord.

This cobra bracelet with the inner strands removed is very similar in size to the double chain sinnet bracelet.

It's a good option if you want a thinner bracelet but prefer the look of the cobra to the double chain sinnet.

Survival Bracelets

Looped Chain Sinnet

The chain sinnet is a very interesting knot. When made with two cords looped into each other you get the double chain sinnet. Both are quick to build and even quicker to take apart.

If you take a look at the four lengths of chain sinnet knots to the right, you can see a pattern. There is a basic overlapping pattern that carries over from the chain sinnet and double chain sinnet.

The third and fourth sets of knots are a little different. They still retain the interior and exterior pattern but have extra inner loops that give the knot more body. By making extra support loops for the main loops to pass through, the knot can be increased in width. It's a slightly more labor intensive process but greatly increases the amount of cord a single bracelet can carry. Each loop adds as much as 7 inches of cord per inch of finished knot.

In section A we'll start by making a bracelet with an extra loop. Then we'll go over working with two loops in section B.

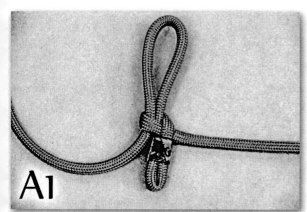

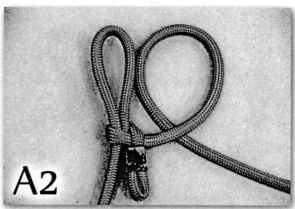

This knot will use about 16 inches of cord per inch of bracelet plus around an extra foot for finishing. Start by setting up the first locking knot above your loop.

Make a loop with your working end by passing the cord behind itself.

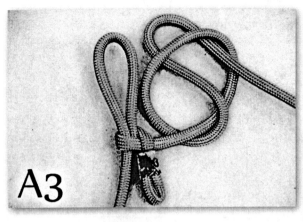

A3

Push the working cord into the second loop, forming a third loop inside the other loop.

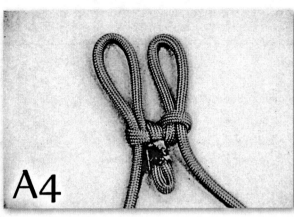

A4

Tighten the second loop down like a knot. It should hold the third loop securely.

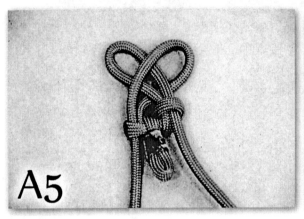

A5

Push the third loop through the first.

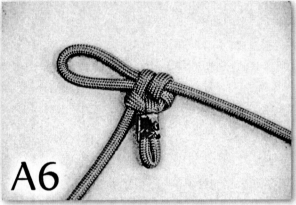

A6

Pull the working end on the left to tighten the first loop.

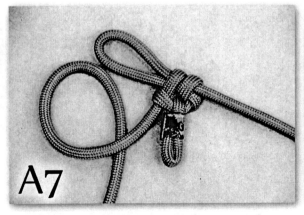

A7

Just like step A2, make a loop with your working end by passing the cord behind itself.

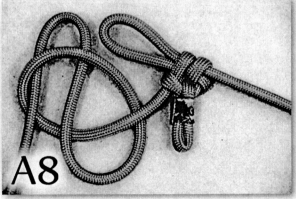

A8

Push the working cord into the second loop, forming a third loop inside the other loop.

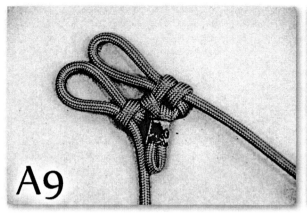

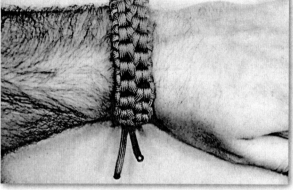

Tighten the second loop down like a knot. It should hold the third loop securely.

Pass the third loop through the first.

Pull the working end on the left to tighten the first loop.

Continue repeating this pattern to complete the bracelet or strap. Finish the end just like on page 117.

This knot adds about 7 inches of cord for every extra loop added to the double chain sinnet. Start by setting up the first locking knot over the end loop.

Make the extra loops by bringing the working cord under itself. Repeat this for as many extra loops you want.

Stack the loops together, bringing each new loop over the previous loop.

Pull the working cord through the loops.

Tighten the extra loops, locking the loop in place.

Push the new loop into the first loop.

Pull the working end on the right side to finish up the first row of loops.

Just like in B2, make the extra loops by bringing the working cord under itself.

Stack both loops, the newer over the older. Then pull the working cord through the loops, creating a new loop.

Tighten the extra loops until the row of loops is even.

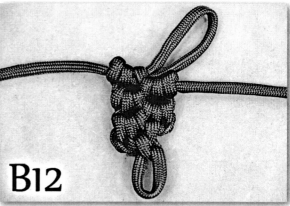

Tuck the new loop into the other locking loop and pull the left working end to tighten.

Continue alternating sides until the bracelet or strap is finished.

Here's a close up of a very wide bracelet with four extra loops.

Survival Bracelets
Taking Them Apart

Now that you know how to tie your own survival bracelets, the next step is knowing how to take them apart.

The most tedious to unravel is the cobra knot. The half knots that make up the cobra hold on to each other, requiring the knots to be opened up by hand.

The double half cobra is much easier to unravel. Its two independent single cord wraps do not connect. Once the core is gone, the knot falls apart.

Finally, all chain sinnet based bracelets and straps come apart easily when the two working ends are pulled away from each other.

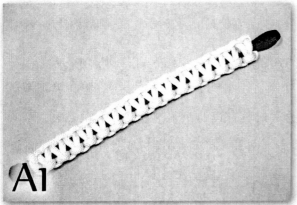

While the cobra knot is one of the more time consuming to take apart, it is still a great knot and stores a lot of cord in a compact bracelet.

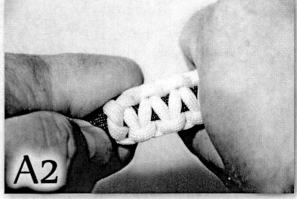

Start by holding the main body in one hand and the knotted or secured end of the core in the other.

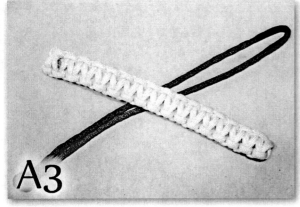

Pull the core out, freeing it from the bracelet.

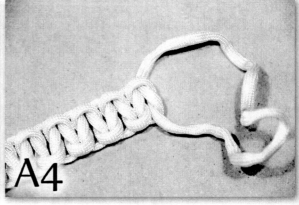

To unravel the cord, start pulling the knots apart. This goes fairly quickly with the core gone.

Once the knot is unraveled, you are left with a nice handful of paracord.

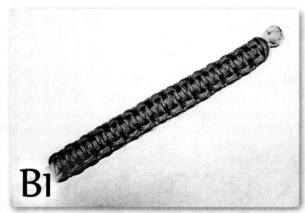

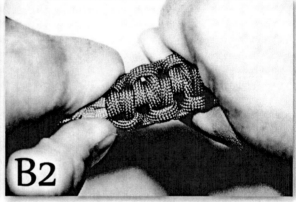

The double half cobra is a great knot for bracelets. It holds a large amount of cord without being too bulky. On the downside, it can be difficult to take apart in longer straps.

To start, grip the main body of the bracelet in one hand and the knotted or secured end in the other. The core is a little harder to pull out compared to the cobra.

Without the core to hold it together, the bracelet will just come apart like a zipper.

You now have a nice little pile of paracord to work with.

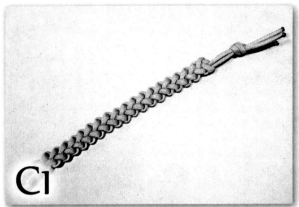

The double and looped chain sinnet are the quickest and easiest to deploy. The knots come apart easily regardless of length, making these ideal for longer straps.

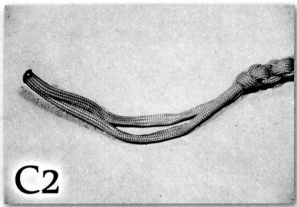

Start by untying the end knot. The bracelet can be unraveled without taking the knot out. If the knot is jammed or you are in a hurry, don't worry about taking it out.

Using the slack between the stopper knot and the chain sinnet, open up the end the cords are tucked into.

Pull the working ends out from underneath the loop.

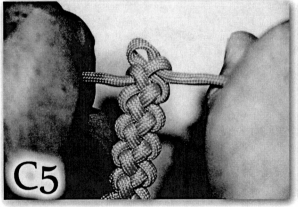

Once the cords are loose, simply pull both sides away from each other. The loops will easily slide apart. Even a long sling or belt comes apart in seconds.

Once the bracelet is unraveled you are left with a nice handful of paracord to use. When you're done with it (if it's in one piece) your bracelet can be rebuilt!

Bracelets and Straps
Straps, Key Fobs, Pulls

Paracord is very tough and durable, plus it's resistant to rot and impervious to the elements. This makes it an ideal material to use for a variety of everyday applications.

Keychains, fobs for keys or larger items, pulls and tabs, straps, and handles can all be made from Paracord. As a bonus, any of these can be taken apart like a survival bracelet to make use of the cord within.

In this section the square braid and round braid will be introduced. While we will go over how to make keychains, these braids can be used for just about anything. They are thick and rope-like, a great way to carry lots of cord in a smaller package.

The other projects in this section can all be done with any knot or wrap.

Straps, Key Fobs, Pulls
Square and Round Braid

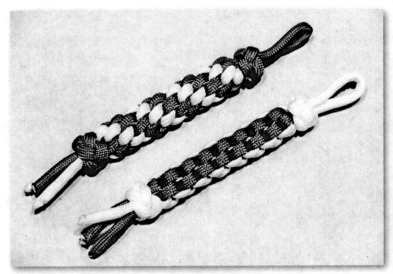

When I was in elementary school, one of the fads was braiding plastic lace. It was during that time I learned how to tie the square and round braids.

The square braid is simply an overlapping weave where each cord in a layer is tucked under another cord. It forms a boxy, square-shaped rope that is fairly compact compared to the round braid.

The round braid is similar to the square braid except that each layer is started slightly off center from the last layer. The result is a stack of squares that spiral to form a braid that is rounded in appearance. It is more like rope than the square braid and is fuller, making it great for knife and flashlight fobs.

These keychains are great for just about anything, and the diamond knot stoppers add up to give them a very clean and finished look. The braids themselves can be used to make straps, lanyards, ropes, and even handle wraps for small items like needle files and awls.

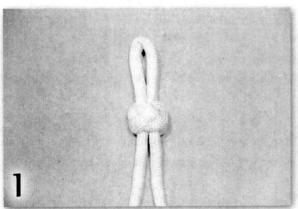

1 Take the center of one of your cords and tie a lanyard or overhand knot to form your loop. The knot isn't required, but makes for a much more finished-looking keychain.

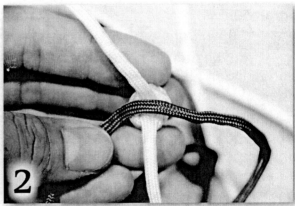

2 Place the other cord across the center of the first cord. I will be referring to the two sets of cords as light and dark cords.

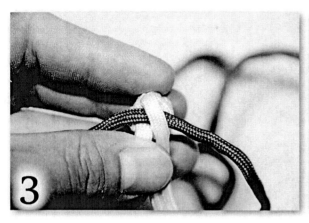

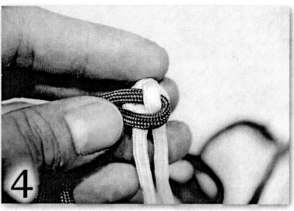

Bring the upper light cord down over the dark cord on the right.

Lay the dark cord on the right over the lower light cord.

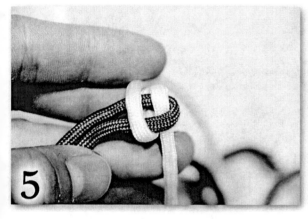

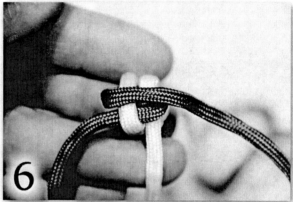

Cross the lower light cord over the dark cord on the left.

Fold the dark cord on the left over the lower light cord. It will be resting on the upper light cord.

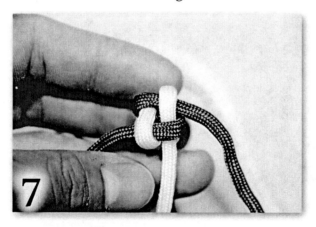

Tuck the left dark cord underneath the upper light cord to complete the first knot.

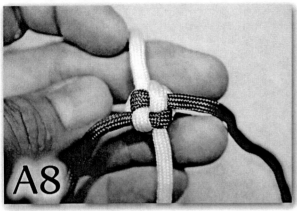

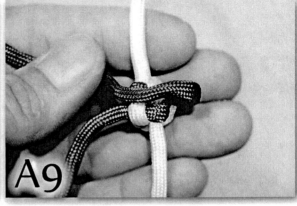

To continue on the square braid, tighten the first knot and keep it straight up and down.

Bring the right dark cord straight over the main body of the knot.

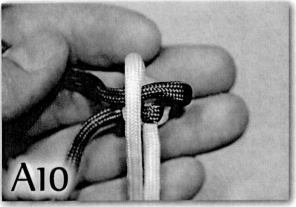

Fold the upper light cord over the right dark cord.

Lay the left dark cord over the upper light cord.

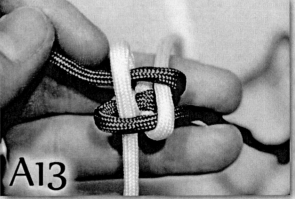

Cross the lower light cord over the dark left cord. It will be laying on top of the dark cord on the right.

Tuck the lower light cord under the dark cord on the right to complete the second knot.

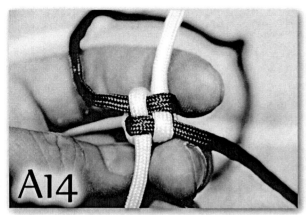

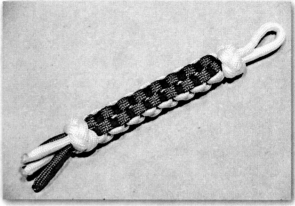

Tighten the second knot. The rest of the square braid is basically a repeat of set A.

Continue braiding until you reach the end. Here is the finished square braid. We'll go over finishing the keychain at step 16.

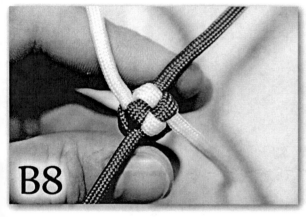

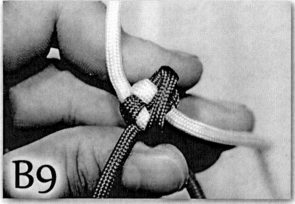

To start the round braid, turn the knot slightly.

Bring the upper dark cord down diagonally across the main knot. It should end up to the right of the lower dark cord.

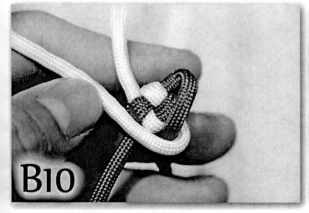

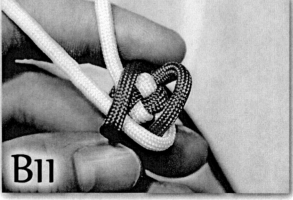

Fold the light cord on the right over the upper cord and slightly below the light cord on the left.

Lay the lower dark cord over the light cord on the left, on the left side of the upper dark cord.

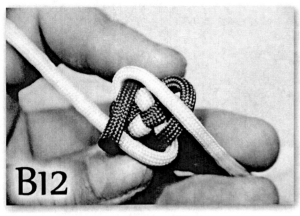

Cross the light cord on the left over the upper dark cord.

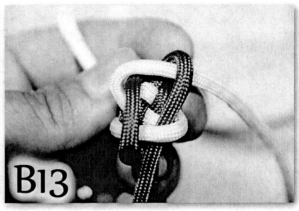

Tuck the light cord on the left underneath the upper dark cord to complete this knot.

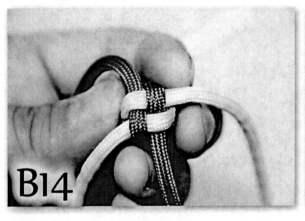

Once the knot is tightened, go back to step B8 to continue the round braid.

This is what the finished round braid looks like. We'll finish the end in the next step.

Once the braid is the right length, tighten the last knot.

Tie a lanyard or overhand knot with two of the four cords. Don't tighten it up just yet.

Pass the other two cords through the center of the knot.

Tighten the knot around the inside cords and make sure to tighten it securely.

Finish the keychain by trimming the loose cords. Because the knot is holding everything together, the cords can be left longer as decoration or cut short and melted flush.

Here are the square and round braid keychains all finished up. Both make great key or knife fobs as well as the ends of lanyards.

They can also be woven from longer cords to make straps or rope. While time consuming, the square and round braids both make good handles for bags and cases.

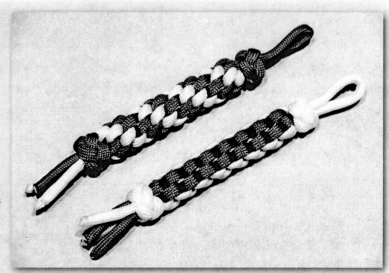

Straps, Key Fobs, Pulls
Single Cord Zipper Pull

When single cord wraps are used to make keychains and straps, they usually come out much thinner than their double cord counterparts. This makes them ideal for thin straps and tabs that can be used to replace zipper pulls.

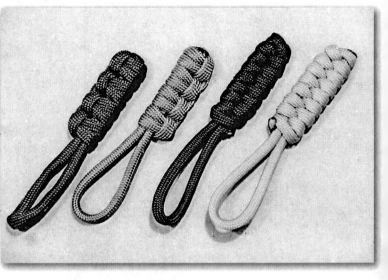

Both knot based and no knot wraps can be used. In section A, we'll make a between bars zipper pull. The same technique can be used to make basic and crossed back pulls as well.

Section B features a half cobra knot. Both the half cobra and helix wraps work and are very easy to do. Since they are knot based, they are very secure and can be started and finished without any additional knots. Knot based wraps can also be applied over no knot wraps in a second pass to increase the size of the zipper pull.

The loops for the zipper pulls can be made adjustable by leaving the starting end longer and tying an overhand knot. That way the loop can be made smaller by pulling on the starting cord and larger by pulling on the loop.

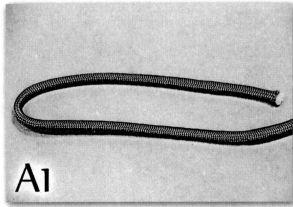

A1

Start by folding over the end of the cord. This will become the standing end, which should sit about an inch from where the wrap will start.

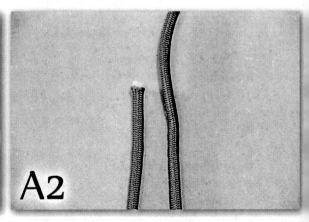

A2

Here are the two ends side by side, the standing end on the left and working end on the right.

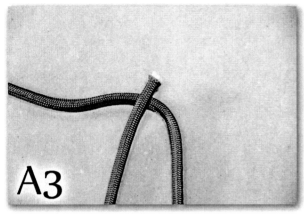

Bring the working cord behind the standing end.

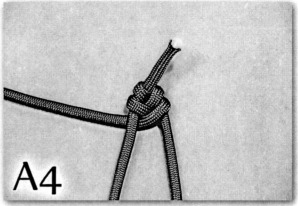

Loop the working end around the front and tuck it under itself to lock the cord in place. Start wrapping around the inner cords.

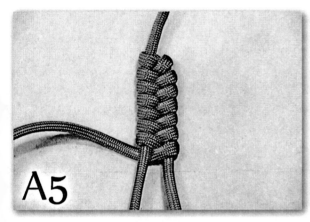

Once the loop is the right size, make sure the wrap is tight and even.

Tuck the cord underneath itself just like a half cobra knot.

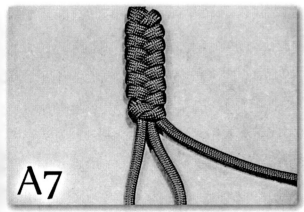

Tighten the knot down to secure the end of the wrap.

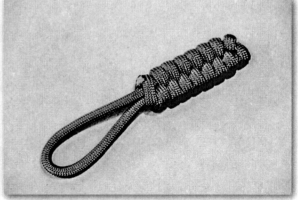

Trim and melt the working and standing ends. Here's the finished no knot wrap zipper pull.

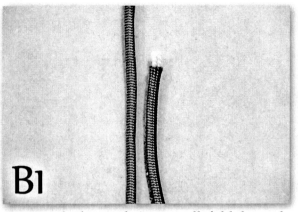

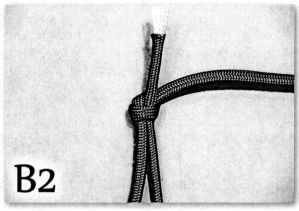

To start the knotted zipper pull, fold the end of the cord over as in step A1. In this case I'm starting with the working end on the left, though the side doesn't matter.

Tie the first knot over the standing end to lock it in place.

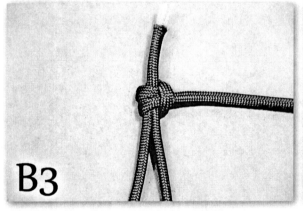

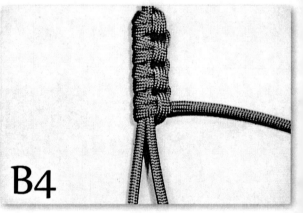

Continue tying knots just like a normal knotted wrap.

Once the loop is the right length, tighten the knot and make sure it is secure.

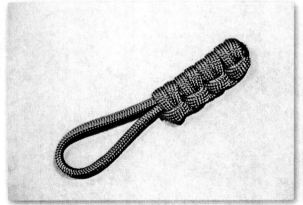

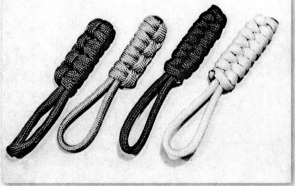

Use your finishing method of choice. The best method for the knotted zipper pull is the knot and melt.

Here are the two styles of zipper pull ready to be attached to a zipper, set of keys or anything else that could use a little bit of paracord.

Straps, Key Fobs, Pulls
Double Cord Key Fob

When using double cord to make keychains and straps, keep in mind that like the single cord zipper pull, a knot of some sort is needed to anchor no knot wraps.

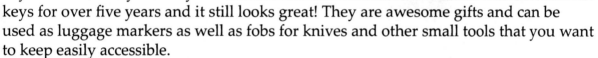

The knot based wrap keychains and straps are very similar to survival bracelets and are great for getting some practice making consistent knots.

I have had the same keychain in this style on my keys for over five years and it still looks great! They are awesome gifts and can be used as luggage markers as well as fobs for knives and other small tools that you want to keep easily accessible.

Both the cobra and double helix make great keychains. The cobra can also be doubled up to make a king cobra, much like the strap on page 141. The double helix makes a really good fob as it is easy to grab. The spiral shape also gives it a good non-slip grip once you do grab it.

Add clips, buckles, and other hardware to make these more versatile.

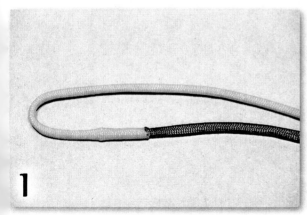

1 Start by folding the cord over at the center. This will become the end loop.

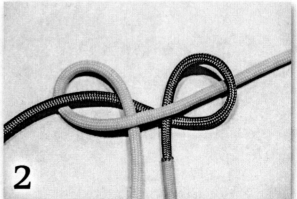

2 Secure the top of the wrap with a cobra knot. This will keep the cord from coming loose and is a good base for any two-cord wrap.

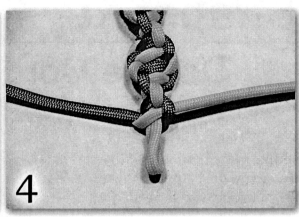

Start wrapping over the two inner cords. Make sure the wrap is tight and both cords are pulled evenly.

Once the loop is the right size, finish the wrap. I personally like tying a cobra knot to lock the ends if I am using a no-knot wrap.

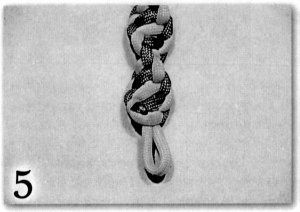

Finish the wrap by trimming and melting the ends if using the knot and melt method.

Here's the keychain all finished up. I like to call the double helix a DNA keychain because of it's shape. It's the perfect gift for the mad scientist in your life!

Here are four keychains, two in cobra and two in double helix. Your keys will never be lonely again.

Straps, Key Fobs, Pulls

Long Strap or Lanyard

Of all the things I have used Paracord for, one of the most used item has been a neck lanyard.

This section goes over how to make a very simple strap with a cobra knot. The size and proportions of this strap can be changed to fit many different needs.

Made with a short strap section and a large loop, you have a neck lanyard. A long strap with smaller loops can become a shoulder strap or sling. By turning the wrap upon itself, integral handles or belt loops can be made.

The strap in this section is very stable and strong, wide enough to keep from twisting, and lays fairly flat. It also contains a very large amount of cord, making it a great way to carry cord with you. That said, longer straps are very tedious to build and take a bit of planning to pull off with minimal waste or without coming up short.

We'll also go over the king cobra, which is essentially a cobra knot over an existing cobra knot. It's a great way to build the strap up in width and thickness.

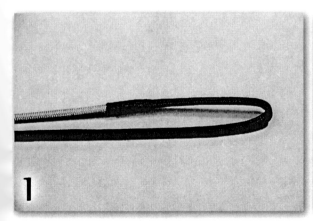

1

Find the center of your cord. If you are using a two cord splice, start with the splice off to the side.

2

Measure out the length of your strap on one of the cords. Make a loop with a knot at the end.

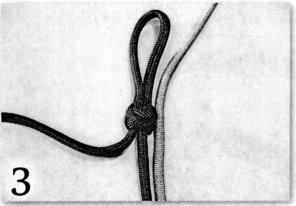

3

Bring the second cord up next to the first. The standing ends will become the core for the strap.

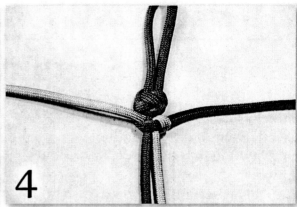

4

Use the working ends and start the cobra wrap like on page 103. Keep some tension on the bottom of the cord so that the cores line up evenly.

5

Once the top knot is set, keep alternating sides and continue the wrap.

6

Wrap until the bottom loop is the size you want it to be. A larger loop makes a good neck or wrist lanyard depending on size.

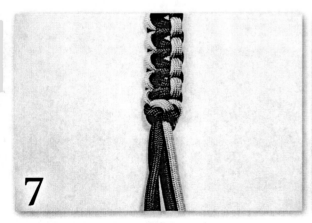

7

Use the loose ends to tie a lanyard or overhand knot over the core.

8

Trim and melt the ends to finish up the knot. Melting will also help keep the knot together.

Here's the finished strap. While it may not look like much, this particular 54 inch long strap used about 50 feet of cord.

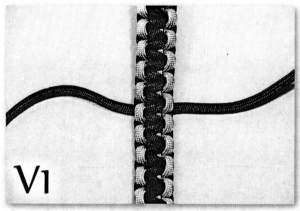

Start the king cobra knot by placing the center of the cord under the strap. I'm using it as a shoulder pad, and it can also be used to both widen the strap and add more cord.

Following the cobra knot wrap on page 67, start the knot. One end goes behind the strap, the other in front. Each end goes into the loop the other makes.

Tighten this to create your first knot. Let this knot fall into the space created by the rows of knots underneath.

Here's the second knot. The knot should end up in the spaces of the knots beneath. Don't try to force it to lay over the high spots or it will be difficult to make the knot consistent.

Continue knotting until the end. The end can be cut and melted or finished like the cobra survival bracelet on page 107.

Here's the finished king cobra. This can be done over any existing cobra knot to add body. It can also be done by flipping a cobra stitch around and going in reverse.

The strap we just built is for an arrow quiver, though it makes for a comfortable and stable strap for just about anything.

The king Cobra works really well for adding extra body to a strap or bracelet.

It's a good idea for making wider handles and for making shoulder pads like on this particular strap.

The basic idea of a long strap can be modified to fit different needs.

The top strap is just a shorter version of the one we built. The center is a neck lanyard for holding keys or a name tag/badge.

The small loop at the bottom was made by tying the cobra back onto itself. This can be used for belt loops or integral handles.

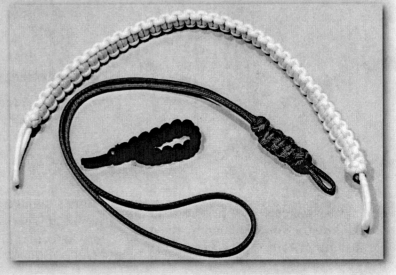

Glossary

Bar - Either a knot based wrap like the cobra knot or the portions of such a knot that cross between ridges.

Cobra Knot - Also known as a Solomon bar and square knot, the Cobra knot is a popular decorative knot. It is the most common knot used for survival bracelets and survival straps.

Core - The core can refer to the inner strands of paracord. It can also be an object that cord is wrapped or tied over.

Full Cord - Paracord that still has its inner strands. Full cord is round in cross section.

Gutted Cord - Paracord that has had its inner strand removed. Gutted or flat cord lays flat.

Jam - This is what happens when a knot under load locks and is difficult to remove.

Kernmantle Rope - A rope that consists of an outer shell (kern) and an inner core (mantle).

Loop - An area of cord where the cord passes itself in a circle. The ends may or may not cross each other.

Mil-Spec - This means that something has been designed and manufactured to military specification and meets required minimum values in terms of quality, materials, construction, and performance.

Nylon - A synthetic polymer with great elasticity and tensile strength. It's rot and water resistant and is used in many different fabric, fiber, and plastic products.

Ridge - The portion of a wrap where two cords are looped or tied to form an area that is raised when compared to the rest of the wrap. Sometimes referred to as the loops in a wrap.

Standing End - The end of a line that is not involved in tying a knot or wrap.

Standing Part - An area of cord between the standing end and the knot or wrap.

Survival Bracelet - A bracelet that is made of a length of woven or knotted cord. If cord is ever needed, the bracelet can be unraveled and the cord used.

Toggle - A stopper used with a loop or clasp to hold two separate ends together. Toggles are used for bracelets, necklaces and lanyards, as well as for holding items closed or together.

Working End - The end of a line that is active or currently being used. Can be called the running or tag end.

Working Part - An area of cord between the working end and the knot or wrap. It is also called the working line or cord and is involved in the knot or wrap.

Bonus Track

The Giant Slayer

The sling is one of mankind's oldest weapons. Simple yet effective in the right hands, it has been used for thousands of years and sometimes shows up in the conflicts of today.

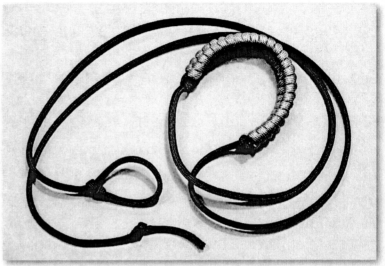

Perhaps the most famous story of the sling is that of young King David and the giant Goliath. In the story, the young shepherd dropped the seasoned warrior with a single stone.

It may seem far-fetched, but make one of these giant slayers and you'll see that the potential of this little length of cord plus a rock is amazing. With enough practice, the sling can be used with steel ball bearings, lead weights, or stones as a means of defense, distraction, and for hunting in a survival situation. This style of sling will even work with larger stones without the woven pouch, giving you the option to use the pouch cord for something else.

Safe practice can be done with golf balls and even marshmallows or gummy candy. A properly sized sling is great for chucking tennis balls too. Have fun!

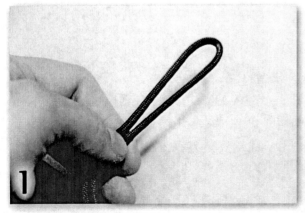

Start by finding the center of the cord. Fold the cord over and measure half the length of your desired pouch. In this case, 2-1/2 inches.

Hold on to one of the cords and pull the other one to increase the length of the loop to the full length of the pouch, 5 inches in this case. One cord will be shorter now.

Take the shorter cord and tie an overhand knot around the longer cord.

Tighten the knot. At this point the loop can be adjusted slightly by pulling the longer cord which will slide within the overhand knot.

Take the longer cord and bring the working end alongside the main loop.

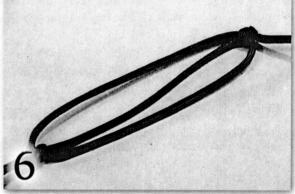

Use the longer cord to tie an overhand knot around the top of the loop. Tighten and adjust the knot so that all three cords are the same length.

Now that the frame of the pouch is finished, start the body of the pouch by taking a 6 foot length of paracord and weave it through the three cords.

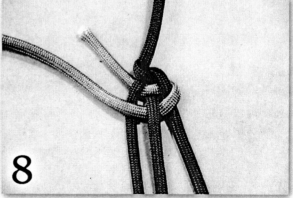

We'll call the light cord A and the dark cords B. The first row will have A go under, over, and then under B. The second row is opposite with A over, under, then over B.

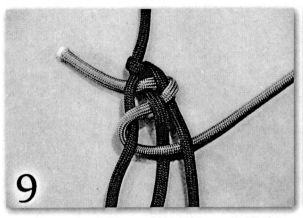

Take the working end of A under, over, and then under B.

Push the weave up to tighten it and lock it into place. This should be done every three or four passes.

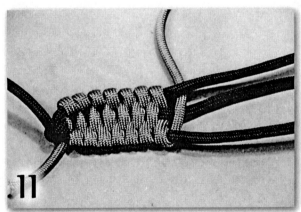

Make sure to keep the cords of B equal. Continue weaving until you reach the end.

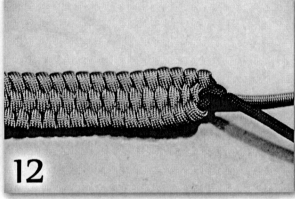

Once you reach the end, use a lacing needle to continue the weave for as long as possible. Stop once the weave is so tight that the needle won't pass through anymore.

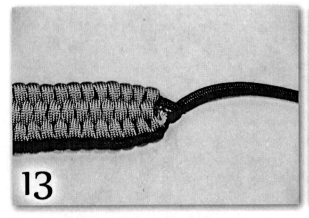

Trim the loose ends to about 1/4 of an inch and melt the ends.

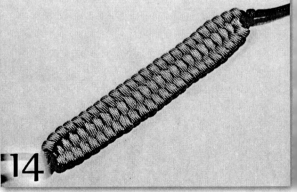

Here's the pouch after weaving. It should lay fairly flat.

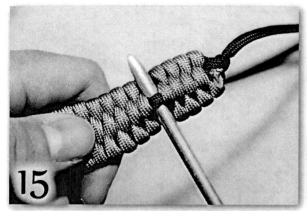

Take a lacing needle or marlinspike and drive it under the center cord of B from the back side. Pull from the end until the cord sticks out.

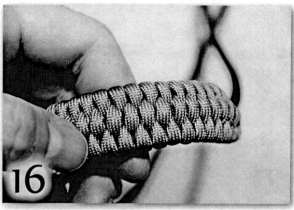

Press the inside of the pouch to shift the cords around. The pouch will start to become more rounded and cup-like.

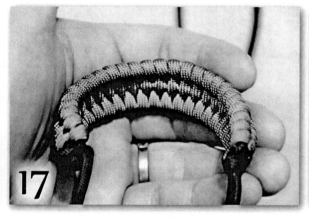

Continue pulling the center and moving the weave until it creates a rounded, cup-like shape.

Here's the finished pouch. The cupped shape holds onto ammunition more securely than if the pouch were left flat.

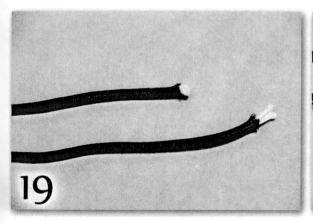

Fold the pouch over and lay the two loose ends next to each other. One may be a little longer than the other.

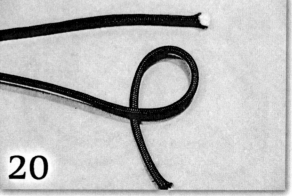

Take the longer cord and make a loop by bringing the end underneath itself.

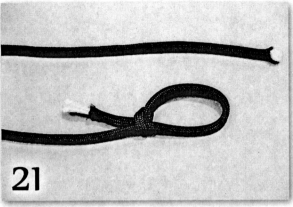

21

Use the working end to tie an overhand knot around the standing end. The loop can be adjusted by sliding the standing cord through the knot.

22

Trim the end of the knot to a 1/4 inch and melt the ends. This will keep the knot secure.

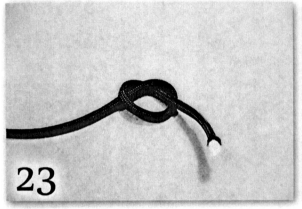

23

Loosely tie an overhand knot near the end of the other cord.

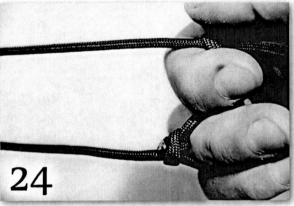

24

Slip the loop over the middle finger of your dominant hand. Hold the knot between your thumb and forefinger, then pull on the pouch to line up the two ends and tighten the knot.

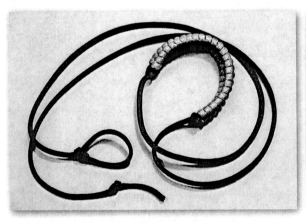

Here's the giant slayer all finished up and ready to sling something! So go ahead, be safe and have fun.

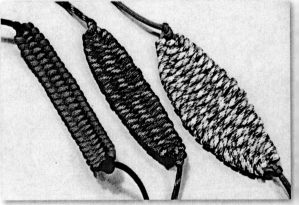

By adding some spacing while doing the weave, you can adjust the size of the pouch. The wider the pouch the more stable the sling is for larger projectiles.